OVERCOMING THE FEAR OF

FLYING

To Reggie –
thanks for your support –
[illegible]

OVERCOMING THE FEAR OF
FLYING

PASTOR EDDIE HARRIS, JR.

Overcoming the Fear of Flying

Publisher:
The Potter's Wheel Book Publishing
eddieharris2212@gmail.com

Published consultant:
Professional Woman Publishing, LLC
www.pwnbooks.com

ISBN: 978-0-578-19651-0

Dedications

To

Callie Mae Tarver-Harris
(my Big Mama, for telling me over fifty years
ago that I could do anything that my heart desired)

The late Eddie L. Harris, Sr., and Mary L. Traylor-Harris
(mom and dad in heaven)

Reverends Micki Michelle Benson and Natalie Renee Lott
(the best goddaughters ever!)

Ronaa Flagler-Ali – sister from another mother
(for typing my first manuscript for Essence
and Black Teen magazines back in 1988)

Susan Taylor – Editor – in – Chief Emeritus, Essence Magazine
(for encouraging me to write this book while
attending the 1996 Essence Festival)

Tracy Jo Edwards – my angel
(for saving my life as I struggled through
heart rehabilitation after my open-heart surgery in 2015)

Foreword

Just living past the age of sixty-five is a gift unto itself, but having someone as a best friend for fifty of them is a gift from God and a miracle to boot. Two outsiders meeting in high school back in 1967, became the driving force that would forge a friendship that without any effort on our part, would last, merely because that's the way God planned it. Eddie and I have been the kind of friends to each other that you don't find much these days; we don't judge, condemn, or talk about each other; we just accept each other for who we are. Even after we both left the military, and returned home to Orlando, Florida, there were times when we never laid eyes on each other for twenty to thirty years; but we always remained best friends. There are many lessons to be learned here, but the most important one is love: love your brother enough to be his keeper!

Pastor Eddie L. Harris, Jr., among other things, is an information sharer. And one critical lesson that God has allowed me to learn as he now serves as my pastor, is that, in life, if you are informed, you can be transformed. I have learned that in order to be informed you must understand how God positions you in your journey. This, my friends, is not rocket science, but the ability to be still and listen to the Spirit of God.

For those of us that truly believe, we understand that even before we were born, God has a plan and it is our job and duty to find that road and lane that we are to follow. In order to do this, we must faithfully believe that God is God and that He will never lie, nor forsake us. He has promised that for those that praise and believe in Him through His Son, Jesus Christ, He will give us the desires of our heart. Do not be blinded by the devil's trickery while walking around with your head in the sand, but lift up your praise, trust God, and soar on the wings of an eagle.

As you read this book, let it be both inspirational and serve as a teachable moment to help you in your journey. And as you journey through this book, you will get a clear understanding of the author, Pastor Eddie L. Harris, Jr., a sincere man of God, and for God and this assignment, he takes very serious. You will come to understand that he understands how God has positioned him and by being humble, obedient, and faithful, and always believing that God would bless him.

It becomes very clear that he is the mate, and Christ is the Captain. For most of us, this is very hard to do, for we think that our plan is the best plan. But beware my friends, for that is short lived at its best. So enjoy reading this wonderful and well-thought out journey, and I leave you with this: how do you line up in your spiritual journey? God bless.

–Larry "Spider" McCalley, Buffalo Soldier of Florida

Endorsements

Have you ever just sat down and took some time to understand the nature of fear? Where does it come from? What triggers it? Is it necessary? Is it worth risking all the treasures awaiting your submission to following God's plan? Is it conducive to the environment of success God has purposed you with? Fear will have you bouncing around the vicissitudes of life like a patient strapped in a straitjacket. But guess what? There is a way out! There is a way to achieve!

If you are looking for your way out and up into the heights of success, have no FEAR! Reading this book will most definitely teach you how to S.O.A.R. You will learn how to:

- Shake fear off and let it go
- Organize your life and get rid of the dead weight
- Announce to the world, that what God has for you is for you and nobody else
- Realize God's plans for your life.

If you are looking for that way out, if you are looking to succeed, if you are looking to overcome your fear of flying, I admonish you to indulge in this masterpiece. It is with the utmost respect and highest esteem that I recommend to you all Reverend Eddie Lee Harris' masterpiece "Overcoming The Fear of Flying (Succeeding)".

–Reverend Natalie R. Lott, M.Div (Temet Nosce)

Captivated and spiritually recharged is how you will feel once you have read Rev.Eddie Harris's, "Fear of Flying (Succeeding). Once you pick up the book, your life will be forever changed by his ability to capture the concept of fear and make it something that people around the world can conquer with practical applications.

–Rev. Micki Reid-Benson, Sacred Sentiments, LLC

"Christianity is the ultimate place of being for so many, but it doesn't negate the fact that, we as Christians, will go through trials and tribulations in this life. The bible says, "For He maketh the sun to rise on the evil and on the good, and sends the rain on the just and on the unjust."

This word from God, OVERCOMING THE FEAR OF FLYING, is that "cure for what's ailing you", that "go to" guide and that "booster shot" that so many need, in times like these.

This book meets you right in that place, where fear can grip your life and leave the believer stuck. It reaches past those barriers of a person's mental defense and self-pity and speaks to their spirit, a word that not only can heal you, but it can release you to SOAR in all that God has for you.

This book is an anointed reminder of whose we are and an anointed guide to getting back to that place of power in Christ Jesus. Blessings to Pastor Harris, for allowing God to use him in such a mighty way, by his being submitted and disciplined enough to bless others through this work of the heart and spirit. After reading this book, there is no excuse, for the believer, not to fly."

Much love to you and your family!!!

–Minister Crystal Brown

It is with great pleasure for me to endorse this well-written book by my long- time friend Reverend Eddie Harris. Each chapter explores deeper into a realm of inspirational adventure. It goes into the depths of the true experience of faith in God.

I'm proud to know that my friend Reverend Eddie Harris is in his season to reap what he has sown!

God Bless...

–Reverend Dr. Pamela K. Fegan Chaney,
Breaking The Chains World –Ministries

Pastor Eddie Harris has written a powerful and insightful book that will inspire and give you a practical "Flight Plan" to Success. This is a must read for everyone who feels like they haven't reached their full potential in God but are ready to experience it NOW!

–Louis M Bell Jr, Founder Kingdom Exchange Ministries,
CEO of Bell Financial Solutions Inc.

Table of Contents

Isaiah 40:31 – "They that wait upon the, Lord shall renew their strength; they will mount up with wings like eagles; they will run and not get weary, they will walk and not faint!"

–ESV

"The wealthiest place in the world are not the gold mines of South America or the oil fields of Iraq or Iran. They are not the diamond mines of South Africa or the banks of the world. The wealthiest place on the planet is just down the road. It is the cemetery. There lie buried companies that were never started, inventions that were never made, bestselling books that were never written, and masterpieces that were never painted. In the cemetery is buried the greatest treasure of untapped potential."

–Dr. Myles Munroe

Introduction

The purpose of this book is to encourage, admonish, challenge and lead the sometimes faint at heart and weak in spirit believer, to continue to hope, wait, and trust and know that God will do exactly what HE said HE would do; while accepting the fact that, there are greater things in store for those who are not afraid of letting go and letting God take you to places you never imagined possible; there are higher heights to ascend, steeper mountains to climb and wider oceans to cross, if only they believe, spread their wings and fly; if only they mount up and soar higher, even higher than the eagles, in Christ, then, they will overcome their fear of flying.

Scripture tells us that, "For God gave us a spirit not of fear, but of power and of love and self-control" 2 Timothy 1:7- ESV. Paul, in his letter to Timothy, admonishes Timothy to remain steadfast in his faith, and to not be afraid to use the gifts that God instilled in him, encouraging him to do the work and will of God, as he understands what need God has of him. For everyone desiring to excel and succeed in life according to God's plan for you, you must recognize that fear alone cannot be made credible, it should not be given a platform by which you succumb, embrace, and nor should you allow fear to clip your spiritual wings of hope in Christ Jesus.

My personal struggle with the fear of succeeding mostly resonated in the crevices of self-doubt. I was plagued with the fear of succeeding for most of my life. I was continually second- guessing myself as I attempted to embark on many wonderful, well-imagined ideas that flooded my soul. Hindsight would reveal that my main problem came cloaked in the form of being too analytical; I put too much time into overthinking the process, and not enough time into trusting God and working through the process.

I soon discovered that focusing on the possible end result more than what was warranted proved to be detrimental to my gifts making room for me. Back then, it never dawned on me that even though I could see myself on the other side of my hopes and dreams, by blotting out the journey through the process put me at a major disadvantage of exercising my faith in God. This was the kind of faith that I desperately needed to appreciate the words of the Prophet, Isaiah; I needed to fully comprehend the power and certainty of the Scriptures, that would ultimately lead me atop the cliff, that would cause me to become more patient, and wait on the Lord; the high place that would profoundly prove to be the place where I would come to fully rely on God; the place where I would learn to spread my wings and soar as an eagle, and victoriously overcome my fear of flying – soaring with the confidence of succeeding in Christ, Jesus.

CHAPTER ONE

Understanding the Nature of Fear

Succumbing to fear is like enduring a "spiritual abortion." Fear can not only maim, hinder, and cause us to down spiral into an abyss of dismal doubt, and shackled spirits, but the truth of the matter is, fear can kill. And the killing is not limited to the obvious reference to dying in the flesh; but fear can and has killed many dreams, hopes, desires, and destinies. Countless persons have seen their whole world turned up-side down, because they could not thwart the presence of fear in their lives. When fear takes hold, it goes beyond the natural, because it operates best in the spiritual – the underbelly of what is of God.

I've heard of too many accounts where individuals spent many years being doped up on prescription and illegal drugs, consumed with uncontrollable eating, suffering from shopping addictions, struggling with bouts of depression and rejection, etc., as they feverishly attempted to rid themselves of low self-esteem, inferiority complexes, doubt, frustration and a profound feeling of fear of either, failing or succeeding, thereby causing them to spiritually abort their God-given destiny.

If we are to truly understand what Paul was telling Timothy when he declared that, "God did not give us a spirit of fear, but of power and love, and a sound mind," 2 Timothy 1:7, then it would behoove us to understand that the very nature of fear is a gift from the devil, our most authentic and unrelenting enemy; the enemy is nothing more than a common thief – one, according to Jesus, "that comes only to steal and kill and destroy." But in that same verse, Jesus reminds us that, "I have come that they may have life, and have it more abundantly." – John 10:10. NLT

Fear is of the devil, and he is our worst nemesis! And I admit that fear can come from two different paths – from within and from without. In other words, fear can be self-imposed and inflicted, or we can allow others to broker fear into our being. However, it doesn't change the fact that fear is not of God, it is from His nemesis, Satan; and by all accounts, fear cannot produce anything that remotely resembles anything that is good, possess real power, (only perceived power), love and a sound mind – those characteristics come only from God.

In my own lived experiences, I can recount instances when God had positioned me for great things – and somehow or another, I was unable to see those things to fruition. There were times when I, perhaps even blamed others for my lack of success, and for my failures, and for my own inability to follow thru on my divine assignments. But, after a while, through self-examination, I began to realize that everybody can't be wrong all of the time. It was some time later, that I accepted the fact that, I had succumbed to the fear of both failing and succeeding. I had determined that the only way for me to succeed was to put all of my energy and trust in my knowledge and ability – only to find out that, without God, I could do nothing.

But, for inasmuch as fear can be readily identified as a menace to God's plan for our lives, it must also be understood that, with faith and trust in our Lord, and Savior, Jesus Christ, fear is not, by its very design, a conqueror; fear only conquers when we yield to its whims;

fear is never an absolute or end all to who we are in God's Master Plan, and what God will ultimately do in the wake of strengthening those of us who yield unto him.

Is it un-natural, or sinful to be afraid? Absolutely not. However, as believers, we should hearken to the admonishments of Christ – "All we need is faith the size of a mustard seed." Luke 17:6 NLT. I often wonder what may have been going thru the mind of Jesus as He chastised the disciples on more than one occasion, to have no fear, only to accept the fact that even though He had trained them, taught them how to perform miracles; even though they had witnessed Him do the impossible, perform the miraculous, they, yet, lacked faith – "But He said to them, "Why are you fearful, O you of little faith?" Then He arose and rebuked the winds and the sea, and there was a great calm." Matthew 8:26 NLT.

I think that this text says a lot about how many Christians line up with their faith and their fears while traveling thru life's journey. Accordingly, there were twelve anointed men on board this boat; taught, trained, equipped and empowered to do the miraculous, and along came a storm, and they panicked. They lost all faith, hope was fading, they were panic stricken, and desperate, and they bothered Jesus. Now what does that say about them? What does that say about many of us?

So what if your boat (life) is taking on water; what about it, that strong winds are filled with trials, challenges, acid tests of life; what about the faith that you professed when the sun was shining on your side of the street? Does having faith enough to overcome fear mean that you only trust God when you are not bothered with having to confront your fears head on?

Now in all honesty, my first reaction to dealing with the unknown, the potential danger that looms ahead, when assessing the insurmountable challenges that are before me and analyzing the odds and impossibilities that I must overcome, I would more than likely react much like the disciples. However, now that I have grown stronger in my prayer life, I've learned to trust and believe in God's Holy Word – and subsequently, I would make a concerted effort to trust in what I know that God has deposited in me, and I would blindly and boldly opt to operate in a spirit of victorious faith, rather than bother Jesus, or call on God first, with whinings of doubt and fear.

And so I ask you, what is it that you are afraid of? What is it that causes you to not fully trust and rely on God to do exactly what He said He would do? What causes your heart to tremble when you think about stepping out of your familiar comfort zone and trusting in God? My brother and sister, I do hope that you don't believe or think that you are the only Christian that has experienced these bouts of fear.

However, it is only the true believers in Christ; it is only those who have come to know that there must be something good about to happen to you and for the good of others, that causes fear, to fear you and the promises that God has laid up for you. As a child of the civil rights movement, I can recount the horror stories that my parents and others shared firsthand, about the hatred, the violence and injustices they had to endure to the delight of Jim Crowism, in order that they may secure a brighter future, and a good life for us.

Were they afraid? Yes, on more than one occasion, but they never gave in to fear, but rather, they were driven by their faith in God, always chanting and singing, "weeping may endure for a night, but joy comes in the morning," always doggedly moving forward in faith, declaring that, "I'm so glad that trouble don't last always." For everyone who has gone thru great trials and tribulations while facing insurmountable odds, while pressing thru the acid tests of life with an undying determination to succeed, each of them have left invaluable life lessons for us to emulate and embrace as we struggle and search for that path towards overcoming the fear of succeeding.

A few years ago, Bishop T.D. Jakes, preached, "You've Got to Go Thru It, In Order to Get To It". Now there's an awesome life lesson for us all. Yes, there will be hindrances, obstacles, deterrents, detours, distractions and detractors that will each cloak themselves in the garment of fear and attempt to derail, destroy and deny your destiny. But today, I declare and decree, in the immortal words of President Franklin D. Roosevelt at his first inaugural address, "the Only thing we have to fear is fear itself!"

In other words, fear really is just a condition of the mind, that for the bold believer, it should never be able to take a stronghold on or in our lives. The bible very clearly tells us that, "I can do all things thru Christ which strengthens me." Philippians 4:13. NLT. And finally, Jesus declared that, "The thief comes only to steal, and kill and destroy, I have come that you may have life, and have it more abundantly." NLT.

This my sisters and brothers, should be the lift-off point where you come to realize that what God has for you, is for you, and no weapon, of any kind, designed, developed and directed towards your destiny in God will ever prosper – now take up your wings and S.O.A.R.; go now, and succeed in all that you think, say, and do!

S – Shake it off, let fear go.

O – Organize your life, get rid of dead weight.

A – Announce to the world, that what God has for you is for you and nobody else.

R – Realize God's plans for your life, because your ultimate success depends on it.

The very nature of fear, is to cause you to abort your God-given DESTINY.

Devotional

Today, I simply declare that I'm confessing to God and a mighty cloud of witnesses, that I'm no longer fearful. I refuse to be scared out of my blessings. I insist on believing that I can remain bold in Christ, and that there's no place for timidity in my faith walk, nor my desire to soar. I am rather matter of factly preparing to spread my wings, and take-off into a life of God ordained success – and there is no demon in hell that can abort my mission; there is only one plan for my life, and it's the plan that God has written just for me.

Prayer

I will have no other God, but the God that sits high, and looks low! I will trust only the God that calls me His child. Father, in the mighty name of Jesus, I will forever hold fast to your unchanging love and pray that you never turn away from me, as I have so grievously done to you in the past. I ask your forgiveness, and pray that you will continue to call out my name, when You whisper, well done, thy good and faithful servant, in Jesus' name, amen.

CHAPTER TWO

This Matter of Eagles

"Strength – We have no sufficient strength of our own. All our sufficiency is of God. We should stir up ourselves to resist temptations in reliance upon God's all-sufficiency and the omnipotence of his might."

–Matthew Henry

When Isaiah inserted the likeness of eagles in chapter 40, I almost missed its significance for the one thousandth time. I've preached and taught from that text countless times, but never, not once, until recently, did I give pause to the matter of eagles beyond how majestic and powerful, and symbolic they are. However, this last time, God brought me to a slow roll and made me take a long, hard look at why He, perhaps imparted the need for eagles in Isaiah's spirit.

I couldn't help but wonder, what was it about the eagle that had so much to do with the renewing of strength; and mounting up with wings similar to his; and where and how do we identify with the eagle when it comes to running and not getting weary, and walking and not becoming faint? I discovered a new-found curiosity about Isaiah's comparison between an eagle and those of us who at one time or another, will grow tired and weary while running this Christian race, as we struggle to find our way to success.

And, I was also able to glean the theological connect between the weakness of the un-repentant sinner, and the equipping, the prowess and the power of the eagle. First of all, I love Isaiah's determination and insistence regarding the matter of turning from one's wicked and sinful ways, and in so doing, him pressing his claims about how, through obedience to God, the sinner can find renewed strength; strength not just in sheer power, but the kind of strength that sustains us when we grow weak and faint, even when we stumble and fall, but strength that causes us to mount up and soar, much like an eagle.

On several occasions, I've seen many a long time believer come and kneel at the altar rail and lament and sob all over the floor, while pleading to God for sweet relief. And it never fails, they almost always, go back to their seats, carrying that same heavy burden of doubt and fear, frustration and un-certainty about what tomorrow will bring. With their shoulders slumped over as if carrying the burdens of Christ, they appear to doubt God's ability to do anything but fail; they even behave as if it's almost impossible to believe that, when they are weak, God is strong.

To run and not grow weary, walk and not faint is a testament to one's belief and understanding that we are a "can't do people, serving a can do God". In other words, without God's help and intervention, anything that we endeavor to do has finite results and minimized power. And sadly, many people don't come to that realization until they are in dire straits; not until after they've tried their best to make matters better, only to give in to the reality that they have created an even greater mess than was ever necessary.

Isaiah, however, attaches sin to failure. And he admonishes the sinner to repent, and come back home to God. He makes it clear throughout his writings, that God is a loving and forgiving God, for those who humble themselves and submit to His will and His ways. And in my most humble opinion, here is where many never get to realize the fullness of all that God has in store for them.

Some have indicated to me that it's hard to give up what they know to exist, for blessings from a concealed God. Usually, this is when God places it upon my heart and lips to remind them that what they have, came from and continues to come from God; God tells us that the earth is His and the fullness thereof. I am amazed at such responses from those that have lived long enough to have a head full of gray hair or no hair at all, and yet, they still find it difficult to fully trust God.

And the overarching question that haunts me, is how long will it take for them to come to their senses and know that God is the giver of all things, big and small, seen and un-seen? What will it take for them to acknowledge that had it not been for the Lord on their side, where would they be? Do they not remember that when life had them by the roots of their hair, dragging them down the streets of despair, that God came and gave them sweet relief, releasing them from the bondage of weariness, even though many of them had not done anything for Him lately?

I am emphatically determined to accept the notion that, even though some of them, while being challenged by the acid tests of life, never embraced the strength and power of God as the way out of no way, as a shelter in the time of storms, as the strong tower in the midst of their weakness. I submit that some people are determined to suffer, and remain faint from struggling and doubting, even though everlasting suffering was not part of God's plan for them and their present situations.

Like the eaglets, God has prepared a place (nest) for each of us to learn, grow, and trust; He has created a space for us to be nurtured by Him and protected from all hurt, harm and danger. Yes, God has created even a secret hiding place, high above all else, for those of us who believe – and yes, we have in Him, a divine exit strategy, an escape route from sin that yields the blessed assurance of being pampered, cared for, loved and forgiven, by the best Daddy of them all – God, Himself. And in my humble opinion, I believe that the use of the eagle as an illustration, is for the sole purpose of allowing us, those that believe, and those that need to become believers, to recognize that, even though the eagle is a bird, it is a bird above all other birds – it can do things that other birds could never dream of doing; the eagle shows us by its very own design, lifestyle, habitat, habits and abilities, that accordingly, through Christ, we can do the same, and in so doing, we can do those things without surrendering to fear, but succeeding in life by trusting the wind beneath our wings to take us to shores we've never seen, meet people we've never known, and against all odds, do the impossible.

Devotional

Sometimes life doles out an extra supply of weariness – family members and friends pass away. An un-expected illness causes a terrible setback that impacts every nook and cranny of our lives. The world seemingly is spinning out of control faster than the speed of thought. And, even though we pray to God with all the might within us, He's nowhere to be found. There's evil running rampant on every corner of the globe, killing innocent people in the name of, being right. Yes, these are the kinds of things that can cause the best of us to grow weary and faint at heart.

However, when we, as Christians, learn how to think like and emulate an eagle, we can overcome life's tests and all that may rise up against us in an attempt to abort our God given destiny. Here is where a careful study of an eagle's prowess, sustainability, and its determination to prevail is very important and beneficial to us all.

It is said that in flight, a Bald Eagle is able to sight a rabbit two miles away. And that with its Talon-eye coordination, from its perch at the top of trees, it can dive at 125-200 miles per hour to catch its prey by its talons. It can also build a nest than weighs as much as 3 tons. And finally, for its sustainability, the Bald Eagle prefers its habitat to be near the water – rivers, lakes, and streams, where the food supply is plentiful.

Saints, there's a lesson in this for each of us. Like the Bald Eagle, we must sharpen our vision so that our eyes can remain on the prize – the goal of becoming successful. Many times what we seek is further down the road than we'd like for it to be, but with eagle like vision, we will never lose sight of what we're after. And there's the matter of not being slow to pursue our dreams – seasons come and go, and if we move too slow, we can very easily find ourselves in a new season, suffering through disappointment and lack, merely because we didn't move with the swiftness and speed of the eagle. Also, never dismiss the importance of small or humble beginnings. Establishing a determination to add to your efforts daily will pay off in the end – who knew that an eagle's nest could weigh as much as 3 tons (6 thousand pounds). Note here, however, that the nest started small with sticks and straw, and other small stuff that the eagles use; and over time, many years, they've erected a mighty fortress for its family. And finally, just as the eagle prefers waterways as its habitat, we, too, must opt to establish our life's goals and ambitions near the water – but, the life sustaining water that I'm recommending, is Jesus Christ, the Living Water – the Author and Finisher of our faith – in Christ, we will never thirst again; in Christ, all things are possible!

Prayer

Thank you, Lord, God – for the gifts and talents that you have instilled in me. Thank you, Heavenly Father for the passion and purpose that You have poured into me. Thank you for, impressing it upon my heart, to have desires of success and significance. And, now, God, give me the strength, courage, and faith, to run on and take flight to do the things that you purposed me to do, as they are done for Your Glory, and our good, amen.

CHAPTER THREE

The Flight Plan

Understanding the flight-plan – a flight plan is a document which provides detailed information about a planned flight. The document is filed with aviation officials, and forwarded to officials at the plane's destinations or waypoint to ensure that they have the data in hand. Filing a flight plan is required by law in many cases, and it is also a good idea from a safety perspective, as it ensures that if a flight goes missing, someone will start looking for it.

Several pieces of information are included in a flight plan. The names of the captain, crew, and passengers are included, along with descriptions of any cargo which may be carried. The type of aircraft is also discussed, as is the type of flight, indicating whether the pilot will be flying with instruments, or under visual flight rules. The flight plan also details the departure and arrival points of the aircraft, the estimated route the plane will take, and the expected duration of the flight.

In addition to providing this basic data, a flight plan also usually details alternate airports which it will use in the event of an emergency. It may also specifically address concerns about controlled or restricted airspace, and other issues which may come up during the flight. The idea is to create a complete picture of what is going to occur on the flight, and to demonstrate that the crew has prepared for unexpected events.

Invariably, many Christians and non-Christians alike, fail to understand that God has a plan for each of their lives. And unfortunately, too many go down the runway of life, lifting off into the wild blue yonder that subsequently turns out to be not so blue; and it is all due to the fact that they did not bother to check in with God to see what plans He had for their lives. This is not to say that there will never be any rough take offs, turbulence and rough landings; however, it does suggest that if we allow God to script, plan and negotiate the flight plan, ultimately, life's flights will abound with success.

Many years ago, God gave me this: "every good leader, must have been a great follower," at the very least a willing follower. I will never forget the invaluable lessons that the military taught me. I've always known that I possessed certain leadership qualities, but I've always attributed it to the fact that I was passionately willing to observe, assess, and follow good leadership. The military recruits, trains and equips individuals to do a job par excellent. And should a soldier in training fail to measure up, several options are offered to assist him/her with corrective action – one of which, and the least favored, is being discharged as unfit to perform military service. In other words, there is a prescribed plan to be adhered to, that has little room for deviation. And even though many a wanna-be soldier may have dreamed of being a professional soldier, ready and willing to serve his/her country, but because they fail to measure up, their dream becomes a dream denied.

But thanks be unto, God! God operates on a totally different system. God is always looking for ways to bless us. And God is intentional about not wanting us to, or letting us fail. But we must be complicit in His quest to bless us into success. Our complicity must be anchored in trusting Him, and believing that He only wants the best for us. God reminds us of this in Jeremiah 29:11 – "For I know the plans I have for you, "says the Lord." They are plans for good and not disaster, to give you a future." NLT. The Message Bible says it this way – "I know what I am doing, I have it all planned out – plans to take care of you, plans to give you the future you hope for."

Understanding that the prescriptive plan of God is the best and only way to overcome the fear of flying (succeeding); it's awesome. After all, success is exactly what God had in mind when He created us in His image. I heard someone say a while back that, "God don't make no junk." Oh, how true that is; Jesus reiterated God's plan when He decreed in John 10:10 – "A thief is only there to steal and kill and destroy. I came so they can have real and eternal life, more and better life than they ever dreamed of." (Message Bible).

I have found that one Scripture in particular to be so comforting and reassuring that God desires to bless me beyond measure; even when I had no clue as to how it would manifest itself, I just know down through the marrow of my bones, yes, all the way down there, that God is working things out according to His divine flight plan for my life. I can only hope and pray that those that claim to know, love and trust God that they are willing to fly by faith and not by what they see through their carnal eyes. For we serve a God that can see way down the road; we serve a God who holds our future in the palms of His hands; the God we serve owns the flight plans and the air space for yesterday, today, and all of the tomorrows to come.

God gives us clarity. God is able to remove the cloak of confusion from around our thoughts, doubts and fears. God can make the most complicated thing become rudimentary; He can break it all down, making it plain and simple for the least of us. Of the many natures of God, and they are endless, one of the things that impresses me immensely about how He goes about orchestrating and planning things, is how He does it without boasting or needing fanfare. No, when God does what He does, the way that He does it, He leaves no room for tampering by anyone – He simply does what He does as only He can do it.

That which was hidden, He reveals it if He chooses to do so. That which was incomprehensible, He presents an appropriate, detailed, flight plan – and, yes, that which requires a divine plan, He's there to clarify as to who, what, when, where, why, and how – our God is a God of Clarity. I believe that once we submit to God's Omniscience through His own words, we will be clear about what He wants us to know: Isaiah 55: 8 – 13 – "I don't think the way you think. The way you work isn't the way I work." God's Decree. "For as the sky soars high above the earth, so the way I work surpasses the way you work, and the way I think is beyond the way you think. Just as rain and snow descend from the skies and don't go back until they've watered the earth, Doing their work of making things grow and blossom, producing seed for farmers and food for the hungry, so will the words that come out of my mouth not come back empty-handed. They'll do the work I sent them to do, they'll complete the assignment I gave them. "So you'll go out in joy, you'll be led into a whole and complete life." NLT.

Beloved – I'm of an uncompromising opinion, that when it comes to doing what God directs us to do, the only thing that matters is that we understand that God has already worked out the details; He's already thought things through; He's already done His due diligence; He's already cleared the runway for our takeoff to success; having already removed any and all obstacles, hindrances, and delays – we simply must get onboard with The Master Pilot – your forecast is Clear and Smooth Sailing ahead – because your flight plan is the *Holy Bible*!

Devotional

Many church-goers are in a constant state of searching for the mysteries of God, as they embark on their quest for success. Searching for a guide, a self-help booklet, etc. However, the looming ball of confusion in too many instances, is that they constantly overlook the *Holy Bible*. It is not unusual for someone to call, text, email, or visit everybody but God, and to no avail, as they proceed to put their plan of success in motion. And finally, when they are struck by the reality that they need to hear a word from the Lord, they sheepishly wonder to themselves, how is it that they forgot about God? *The How to Guide for Success*, has always been the single most working document that has never failed us, and never will, because it is none other than, the *Holy Bible*; one of the least read, but most helpful books by many self-confessed believers.

When read with understanding, the Bible has a prescriptive ability to demonstrate to each of us, how we should live, love, forgive, and honor God. God was very generous when it came to disclosing the mysteries of the how's, when's, where's, and why's, and who's of life. In other words, whatever it is that we determine that we need in order to overcome life's challenges of being successful, God has a unique and specific plan designed for each of us – His plan for our lives is perfectly assigned and retrofitted to guarantee that with Christ, we absolutely cannot fail – success is in our hands. Scripture – Philippians 4:13 – tells us that, "I can do all things thru Christ, which strengthens me!" KJV.

Prayer

Today, God, my pressing need to know all about myself in a micro-minute, has come to an end. I'm no longer on a quest to find you and your mysteries with every waking moment – I've since come to understand that You are quite capable of finding me whenever you so desire, my task is to be in position and prepared when You seek me. Thank you for the clarity of the Flight Plan for my life – I am eternally grateful for your love for me, amen.

CHAPTER FOUR

Travel Light

I have been flying on air planes since February, 1970. And one of the things that struck me as so ridiculously curious, is why is it that the majority of passengers that fly, tend to bring on board the plane so much carryon baggage? I mean, I understand that people need to carry the necessary baggage that they have determined that they will have need of, but seriously, does it really take all of that? When you factor in the time and hassle that goes into dragging all of that extra baggage onto a plane, taking up precious time, and the fact that it is always an inconvenience to the other passengers that are trying to get comfortably seated; it is no wonder the airlines have decided to charge for extra carryon baggage.

I used the above illustration to make a point about how we, as a culture, place such a heavy significance on carrying more baggage around than we really need. In a highly competitive society, or world for that matter, we are inundated with the need for extra baggage – stuff that weighs us down unnecessarily.

And to further substantiate my position, I would like to point you in the direction of three main areas of life where our quest to be successful is often impacted negatively by the extra, unnecessary baggage that we too often carry with us as we eagerly strive towards our hopes and dreams for success.

In each scenario that plays itself out whenever and wherever you hear people talk about why they didn't pursue their dreams of accomplishing some achievement in life, almost always, it has something to do with, people, places and things – these three baggage factors always weigh heavily as the reason or justification for many unfulfilled dreams; the dreams deferred and the dreams denied. There is a fourth factor, but I will save it for discussion near the end of this chapter, stay with me, it may very well surprise you.

I cannot think of anyone that I've ever met, who doesn't have enemies, haters and naysayers. That's just the way of the world. However, what looms over many of those same people, is the matter of not being able to determine with any degree of exactness as to who is for you and who is against you at any given time. Most detractors enjoy hanging around you to steal, kill, or destroy your dreams because they don't have any of their own. And, to complicate the issue, is our desire to be affirmed by someone that we've grown to trust, and emulate.

Too often we don't realize their jealously, envy, and corrupt motives until they have done extensive damage to our emotions and psyche. These are some of the most difficult setbacks to bounce back from. Think about it for a moment – people that you have shared your innermost secrets; people that you've poured your deepest desires into; people that you thought were the protectors of your passion for doing great things with this life that God has given you, only to discover that they were in your life to take from you, while having no desire to reciprocate or support your endeavors. These are the people that have been there for you all along, or so you thought. These are the people, many of them, that always clapped the loudest and the hardest whenever you appeared to be attempting to do something life affirming, so long as it didn't take away the spot light from what they were doing. These are the same people who always smiled in your face and pat you on your back with expressions of approval – or were they?

These are the people that have dug in with their heels and found a roosting place, a stronghold in your corner of the world, for as long as you had something that they wanted, they were there in support of your efforts. And the sad commentary is that we allow these people to take from us time and time again; we permit them to use up so much precious time, time that should be committed to doing the work of a success driven idea or ideal; they used up time that cannot ever be replaced. Yes, these are the people that smile in your face and talk about you behind your back; and they are the ones that would no sooner stab you in the back, rather than see you succeed; these are the very people that follow your every move, but they have no intention of walking a mile in your shoes. But, beloved, that's ok, too; your job is to treat them with the rear window effect – in other words, as long as they are behind you, let them do as a strong wind would do – let them continue to propel you into your season and purpose of success in God. Because as long as they are behind you, they cannot hinder you; what's in front of you, down the road a piece, are the promises of God; promises that He planned for you before you even drew your first breath of life.

But I have come to realize that once we are determined to lean and depend more on God and not others, we positon ourselves to receive what God has been trying to tell us all along – and that is, some people don't mean us any good; they never did and they never will. And, yes, there are those who can't accept the fact that God has a divine plan for our lives that just won't look like the plan that He has for them – and for that one reason alone, they are going to hate you and be very jealous and envious of you. Once we are in position to hear the clear, precise, intentional voice of God – God will tell us to, Travel Light – dead weight will not only weigh you done, but if you're not careful, it will rob, steal, and even kill your potential for success. By whatever measure and means possible – you've got to let some people go, and let them go for good.

One of the hardest and most challenging things I faced once I had fully submitted my hopes and dreams unto God, was my desire to go and hangout in some of the places that I used to frequent, just so that others could see the change that had come over me. Yes, I'll admit it was perhaps a bit selfish, but my intentions were pure. I was happy glad for my peers to see how wondrously blessed I had become through the willingness to surrender my all to the Father.

But a strange thing happened as I pushed to expose this new man in an old environment. The problematic was not how I was received or perceived, but rather I noticed that I didn't feel the sense of belonging, or familiarity that I had assumed would exist. To be perfectly honest, I felt a keen sense of helplessness. I had a trouble in my spirit that caused me to literally shake in my boots. I felt a sense of loss and detachment. Even though I was with friends, family, colleagues, God caused me to come to the understanding that, oft times, like people, places I used to go, would no longer feel right; those places would no longer be able to define me in a sentence or paragraph; those places had a history and a reputation that referred to and described, and to a larger sense, in many ways defined the old me – and for that, they, too, had a weightiness about them that I could not afford to carry forward in God's divine plan for my life's successful journey.

Places sometimes are the only reference point that others commonly remember and refer to as, "those were the days." I can laugh now, but not too long ago, I remember sharing with some church members about how when back in the day, I would be at the club doors waiting to open up, and joyfully exclaim with a ridiculous outburst of verbal pride how I also was on many occasions, was there to help close the club down. But I recall one of the saddest things while I was hanging out, partying in places both near and far. I remember that I was in my early to mid-thirties, but sadly, there was one poor soul, who had to be in his late 50s to early 60s, who was one of the ones that was right there with me from opening to closing. Admittedly, I didn't give it much thought back then, but as I look back over my life, and as I more clearly think things over, I have come to the belief that he must have had to have been a very lonely and sad man. A man in search of something that could not be found in the place where we would come on the weekends to assuage and massage our, "wish I woulda, coulda, shouldas," with alcohol, dancing and pretty women. I shared this particular story to illustrate something real and very hazardous to anyone who desires to accomplish something meaningful with their life – I came to know this person solely by the place where we hung out. He was well employed, he had a wife and family, he had some material accumulations, but he really wasn't going anywhere beyond the dance floor and barstools that he occupied during the eight years that I shared with him.

Because I know him personally, I can tell you that he ended up divorced, lonely, and all alone – and he didn't have to have such an unhappy ending. However, the take-away for us, is that, we both were carrying around a lot of unnecessary weight called, a place; memories, adventures, experiences, relationships, etc., all summed up in a place that led to nowhere. And the missing component was we turned to everything and everybody, except God. But, as for me, because I can't speak for him, my sense of discernment made it known to me that God had a purpose for me that was far greater and much better than what I had been exposed; a place called nowhere – it's a heavy load that absolutely must be laid aside. You will never be able to spread your wings and fly, as long as you're dragged down down with the weight of places that God has determined that are not in your best interest – close the door, lock it, and throw away the key, never to enter again.

It is without question, that we live in a very materialistically driven world. And many of us are defined by the accumulation of things, be they money, cars, houses, property, exotic animals, rare coins and paintings, clothes, etc. However, I have come to the conclusion that the most precious commodity that anyone could ever possess is, "peace of mind." Peace of mind is God- sent. The Bible tells us that we can have a peace that surpasses all understanding. In other words, God is willing and able to bless us with a sense of gratefulness and humility that will keep each of us in perfect peace, even when the storms of life are raging against us. These are the storms that tend to weigh us down with doubts and fears about things that we don't understand or that we lack the ability to determine certain outcomes.

The Bible asks in Matthew 16:26 – "For what is a man profited, if he shall gain the whole world, and lose his soul?" NLT. This is an age old question that we have not managed to correctly respond with any degree of progress. What I am saying here, is that as humans, we suffer with this insatiable appetite to acquire things – things that really only satisfy a temporary, temporal, test of greed. Yes, greed; it seems as if the more we get of something, the more we want. In all too many instances we hear of times when television advertisers tell us that the next big thing is here.

And needless to say, the big thing that you already have is basically brand new, barely broken in, but because there's another, newer model, big thing coming down the pike, you find yourself salivating to have it – and in most cases if not all, there's a catch. And that catch is, what is it going to cost me? Can I really afford it right now? Will it interfere with my financial plans that are already established? Do I really need it, or do I just want to be able to brag about being one of the first to have it no matter what the cost?

Making unwise decisions have always played a major role in causing us to lose focus and getting off track with our plans and God's plans for us to become better tomorrow than we are today. These decisions can and will have a ripple effect on our lives that can and will impact our moral character and our spiritual sojourn, and the lives of everyone connected to us in one way or another. Where and what we place value on will surely determine where and how we end up in life.

Our value and focus should remain on God – serving Him as best we can with our whole hearts, our minds and our souls. Joshua 24:15 states – "Now, therefore, fear the Lord and serve Him in sincerity and truth; and put away the gods which your fathers served beyond the River and Egypt, and serve the Lord. If it is disagreeable in your sight to serve the Lord, choose for yourselves today whom you will serve: whether the gods which your father served which were beyond the River, or the gods of the Amorites in whose land you are living; but as for me and my house, we will serve the Lord." NLT.

In other words, not just any old decision is required here, but rather, a decision that will make all the difference in the world as it pertains to your success or failure – you can't do what others used to do or are still doing for that matter, particularly if it is not of God. While I do realize that there exist certain trappings of this world that will certainly deceive you into thinking that you have become successful and you have finally arrived at a station in life called success by man's definition.

For example – our culture informs us that if you have large sums of money, you're banking, you're rolling in dough; and for that matter alone, you are defined as successful, you've arrived; while all the while, money in and of itself does not make you successful. I believe that what you choose to do with your money determines your success or failure in life.

Some folk think that just because many people live in large houses (mansions) with more space they will ever need, that they are happy and filled with everlasting joy. Many statistical reports have revealed that more families than you think are living a life full of lies and pretentiousness. Those well-manicured lawns, spacious rooms, and over-sized driveways, cannot ever define success in God's eyes – at best, they merely reflect your ability to amass things, and if they are not things of God, they are burdensome things that weigh you down – travel light.

I mentioned at the beginning of this chapter that I had four points that I would share with you that would definitely have an impact on your quest for success in life. And of all four, this last one is the one that has the greatest potential of determining whether you fail or succeed – the last point is, "YOU."

How you access and operate your faith in God is the ultimate determining factor of your success or failure – yes, your faith, if handled properly and with care, can take you to places you've never been. Your faith will cause things that you've dreamed of and hoped for to come to pass. The Bible says, "Fret not yourself because of evildoers, neither be envious against those who work unrighteousness (that which is not upright or in right standing with God). For they shall soon be cut down like the grass, and wither as the green herb. Trust (lean on, rely on, and be confident) in the Lord and do good; so shall you dwell in the land and feed surely on His faithfulness, and truly you shall be fed. Delight yourself in the Lord, and He will give you the desires and secret petitions of your heart." (Psalm 37: 1 – 4) Amplified Bible.

What is being stressed here, is the fact that God will honor your faithfulness by answering the desires of your pounding heart. You, and you alone can succeed in all of life, should you decide to be faithful to God. All you need to do is shed yourself of whatever dead weight that is holding you down – jealously, envy, grudgefulness, and fear from evilness; each of these can weigh you down as you press forward towards a successful outcome in life.

All God requires is that you remain faithful to His commands, thusly, delighting yourself in Him. A few years ago, about twenty-five to be exact – I coined a phrase: "Architect of Your Own Agony." All this means is that sometimes, we are the reason that we don't get out of life what we desire, because often, we are the problem, and not anyone else – You do not have to be the architect of your own agony; however, you can be the architect of your success – speak truth to power and travel light.

Devotional

An un-necessary heavy heart, a burdened down spirit, and sagging shoulders from carrying around the weight of the world, from worrying about things of which you have no control, will take you to an early grave, while leaving countless opportunities and blessings un-realized. Sometimes we become so beleaguered from taking on projects and problems that really should have been passed on to someone else, but our need to get things done causes us to behave as is no one can get it done but us; surely, we're not that in disposable. And the down side to it all, is that what we really should be focused on is our own goals and ambitions that have been left alongside the highway of, "I'll get to it later." Beloved, if you're not careful, "later" may never come – "later" just might be too late. I believe that when God has poured our purpose and passion into the cup of life, we should govern ourselves with what I like to think of as, "the urgency of now!" I may be wrong, but I don't believe that God is desirous of waiting around on us, when we've determined that procrastination and indifference is our mode of operation. Too much stuff to handle; too many things to shoulder that don't belong; too much wasted time; too many misplaced priorities – these are major contributors to weighing us down – these are the things that can thwart our progress towards success by causing us to grow weary in well doing – in all things, travel light.

Prayer

Dear, God – from this moment on, I pledge to surrender my all to thee. I will gladly submit my will, my ways, my hopes, my dreams, my aspirations and my heart's desires to you, so that you can show me the right way, as you so willfully and lovingly shoulder all of which I cannot carry. I release myself from the need to do it all, as well as the desire to prove that I'm capable of carrying the heavy loads, even if they're not mine to carry. Dear, Lord – strengthen me, and give me greater clarity, that I may be able to better focus on my pursuit of continuously pressing towards the mark for the prize of the high calling of God in Christ Jesus – which is for me the ultimate success – the success that causes all other success to be, and to have meaning, both on earth and in heaven, amen.

CHAPTER FIVE

Getting Bumped – When your plans are not God's plans

Remember when you dotted every I, you crossed every T, you checked your list once, twice, even three times, and you had it in your mind that you were all set to go. You even notified the post office to hold your mail, and informed the newspaper publisher to hold delivery until you return at a specified date? Everything looked right and felt right, too.

And just like the happy, excited, all rearing to go passenger at the airport, the next thing you know, due to circumstances beyond your control, life just bumps you. Your plans have been forced to take an uncertain backseat to a situation of higher priority and greater urgency than your plans. Wow! Now what do you do with yourself? If you're like me, to say that you're irritated would be an understatement of the censored kind.

It is times like these when we desperately need to rely on our faith in God to usher us into a greater understanding as to why. Times like these are certain to test and even challenge our faith – is it faith in every kind of weather? Or is it fair weather faith? The kind of faith that you have when everything goes according to plan, the kind of faith when the sun is shining on your side of the street, the kind of faith that you have when you think that you don't have a care in the world.

Now, as for me, I've come into an understanding that caused me to realize that while God may choose not to reveal in specific terms why He does what He does, that if I pay close attention, I can see all kinds of illustrations to help me out quite a bit. As a matter of fact, I remember a story that I heard many years ago about an organ grinder and his peanut loving monkey.

The story goes on to state that back in the day, there was this New York City, organ grinder. And on one particular day this organ grinder and his pet monkey were on a street corner, entertaining children and families as they passed by. It seems that on this particular day, the organ grinder was waiting on a shipment of peanuts to be dropped off at that same corner. While waiting on the shipment of peanuts, the monkey was unusually disinterested in the passersby and was more preoccupied with a container of peanuts that the organ grinder had brought along to give to the monkey sparingly as they waited.

Well, after a few hours had passed by, the monkey decided to sneak the entire container of peanuts and scuttle into a corner and feast on them. Without the watchful eye of the organ grinder, the monkey crammed his hand into the jar and commenced to grab a handful of peanuts just in case the organ grinder caught him and took the peanuts away from him. However, it was right about that time that the peanut delivery man showed up with bushels and bushels of peanuts. The monkey jumped with excitement, making all kinds of animated noises of gladness. But soon he grew frustrated because he couldn't free himself from the jar of peanuts that he had stolen – his plan was backfiring on him. You see, saints, while he had a fistful of peanuts, he was so caught up on not releasing the few that he had in order to get his hands on the unlimited supply that had just been laid at his feet.

It would appear that the monkey didn't want to relinquish the good thing that he held in his hand in order to take advantage of the GREAT blessing that had just been dropped at his feet; he was **unsuccessful** at being able to tap into the abundance that was his for the taking. I hope that by now you have gleaned several lessons in this story, but my prayer is that at the very least you grabbed hold of this one: God realizes all that we've put into planning our lives, coordinating the logistics, and specifying times, places and things, however, God knows what's best for us – and even when we're living a fairly righteous life, God still knows what's best for us – but in order to be able to receive the abundance that God has ordered, we must be willing to let go of the adequate.

With God, you may often find yourself being bumped – but the joy in being bumped by God is being reassured that God has something better in store for you because you are His seed, and He determines your growth, He alone Has the power to facilitate a divine, successful outcome for your life.

Unfortunately, many well intended, I'm next in line for a miracle, it's my turn, I can't wait Christians, allow their impatience to become their blessing blockers. Think about it for a minute; you're standing in line at the airport with ticket in hand, your bags already on the plane, and all that you want to do is board the plane, get comfortable and superimpose yourself into your journey's end. And all of a sudden the ticket agent calls you up to the counter and ask you if you would mind giving up your seat for someone else, or perhaps, or maybe you're told that the plane is overbooked and they need several passengers to relinquish their seats with the promise of free tickets, complimentary hotel stays, etc.

Now we all know that this scenario can go one of two ways – and it all depends on your outlook. If you have that, no way, no how, attitude – I'm getting on this plane and I don't want to hear another word about it – or, if your attitude is flexible and you can see the benefits (blessings) in the offer, because your attitude is what the order of the day calls for – you are compensated abundantly for your cooperation; isn't it a great feeling to know that you can be compensated handsomely for just a little inconvenience? Well, that's the way it is with God – sometimes God wants you to step back and let Him be a blessing to someone else, with the promise that He will give you more than you could ever imagine for your trouble.

True enough, your first inclination may very well be that you're not up to being asked to step to the back of the line, or to give up your sure thing that you feel that you have every right and privilege. I understand that and I empathize with you more than you may realize. However, I have never seen God break a promise, and I have never encountered a lie that He ever told. Being bumped, or denied something that belongs to you, sure, who knows, in addition to being rewarded, sometimes God is trying to keep you out of harm's way – for your own good. More prominently, when God bumps us – God is merely echoing His promise, that the last shall be first, and the first shall be last – it just all depends on your attitude towards the process.

About ten years ago, I preached a sermon entitled: "Your Setback, Is A Set-up, For Your Comeback!" I really love that sermon for more reasons than a few. Actually, I lived that sermon, and continue to do so even today. I have always been overlooked, by-passed, sent to the back of the line – but each time, God would always reward me for my submissive attitude unto Him.

Here I am, way past the age of fifty – having successfully overcome a series of being "bumped," and God still has His mighty hands upon my life, while making good on every promise that He ever made. God promised me that I would be the head and not the tail – I am a joint heir of a royal priesthood – I am a child of the King – bumped, bruised, beaten, battered and betrayed, and yet I'm victoriously bound for success. I am His and He is mine. My brothers and sisters, if you are serious about jumping out into the deep end of life; and you are determined to succeed at whatever your endeavor – if you really want to be successful in life – just remember that being bumped every now and then is not the end of the world – you must simply never forget whose you are, and that Father knows best!

Devotional

There are countless stories about people who were denied an opportunity that they had coveted for great periods of time, only to have someone they trained, or taught, get promoted ahead of them and receive what they passionately considered to be, their promotion. This is a very disappointing and hurtful thing to have taken place for anybody, especially for the Christian, whose faith is being tried. It becomes problematic in part, because there's the tendency to question God as to why they got bumped. But in that same scenario, stories have been shared about how within ninety days down the road, the company had a major shake-up with cutbacks, layoffs, and downsizing, etc... – yes, you guessed it; that coveted positon was one of the first to go, but your current position was one to be secure – you got bumped, but God kept you out of harm's way, and your job security and ability to remain financially stable, went un-interrupted – we bless, God today for His Omniscience, we call on His name with a grateful heart, in humble submission, we say, thank you Father – for You know far better than we, not only what lies ahead, but surely, what is best for us.

Prayer

Hear us, Dear God, when we cry out for direction. Please don't allow temptation to overtake us with pride and a sense of entitlement, just because of what we have in our possession. Father, give us the strength, wisdom, and humility to know that in You, sometimes we must be made to understand that when You desire to bless us, we must release from our possession those things that prevent You from replenishing us with more and better blessings. Strength to give up something, in order that we may be able to receive what you have already earmarked in heaven with our names on them, this is my prayer, as I move over, and make room for You, amen.

CHAPTER SIX

Stand-By (In the meantime)

Who in their right mind wants to be required to wait, when they are desperately trying to get somewhere, and in a hurry at that? Because of who I am, and my penchant for wanting to get to where I'm going without interruption, flying stand-by has never been an attractive option for my air travel plans. Listen, what good is an airline ticket if it can't guarantee you a seat on the plane – a flight for which you paid for, but, however, with stipulations? I can remember back when I first started flying, which was ions ago, how stressed I became as I sat there in the airport terminal listening to the representative at the check-in desk call everybody's name but mine. I can remember telling myself that one day, I won't ever have to be put on stand-by again. Oh, how wrong I was! Clarification – yes, I can now afford to purchase an airline ticket other than stand-by; but my reality check came when God showed me that in life and living, there will be times when I would have to learn to WAIT on Him! God showed me that, with Him at the helm of my pursuits, there is value in waiting.

I've come to understand that there is a Ying and a Yang in waiting. What I mean by that is when waiting, there is a natural tendency to super-impose our own imagined possibilities into the process – in other words we find ourselves calculating and strategizing about the potential outcomes that can be had. While on the other hand, because waiting has more to do with factors that we have no control over, we find ourselves panting and panicking over the mysteries of waiting – I've always believed that when God is silent, He's up to something.

Scripture tell us that, God's thoughts are not our thoughts and His ways are not our ways; God and God alone bears ownership to both the Ying and the Yang of our lives. And who we are, and who we are to become, inherently is determined by God, but whether or not this should ever come to pass, rests heavily on our willingness to exercise our free-will properly – oddly enough, God has this strange thing about Himself that causes Him to be cautious about imposing His Will on us, particularly when we are being ridiculously obstinate and disobedient. He will however, allow us to waller and crawl in the misery of waiting on Him to bless us into success as we find ourselves in a place called, "in the meantime," – a place for stand-bys.

A bad or miss-guided attitude can be the very reason that many success stores never get born or written, they simply die in the minds, wombs, and hearts of the hopeful – if you are impatient, refusing to stand-by, if you choose to lean to your own understanding rather than putting your faith and trust in God, if you try to rush God by attempting to get ahead of Him or make crucial decisions without conferring with Him, then I can assure you that the success that you seek will forever remain an elusive mystery, buried in the tomb of impatience.

Waiting requires patience, and the Bible says that patience is a virtue – admittedly, waiting on God can prove to be challenging, however, the rewards always out-weigh the patience and pains poured into the waiting. God has a habit, by design, of being very intentional about how He needs us to handle our stand-by situations in life. I know personally, that God desires us to wait in humility. Some years ago, as I struggled to pursue my dreams of becoming successful, God intervened and showed me that it wasn't a negative thing to wait in humility. As a matter of fact, I can recall Him whispering in my spirit this phrase: "humility is power under control." God made it plain to me that, if you surrender your whole-self unto Him while you wait, you have access to God in a way that is for the most part, completely un-explainable.

Society, sometimes shackles us with the thought that if you are humble you're weak. But in actuality, and think about this for a moment; if you are connected directed to God, you get to share in His power thru the divine opportunity of full surrender through the process of humility. But for those who are determined to go it alone without the power and protection of God, you will soon find out for yourself that God orders all steps, and any other steps that are ordered other than His are destined to fail, with God's wrath and indignation.

As a matter of fact, several Bible stories come to mind when I think about God's response to the necessity to stand-by and wait for His response. I remember the story about Cain and Able – where in Genesis 4: 3 – 6, when both Cain and Able brought their offerings unto God. Here is a very good and often missed divergent perspective on this text. From God's perch and perspective, He waited for them both to bring forth their offerings – Able, on one hand, kept flocks, and Cain worked in the soil. Abel's offerings consisted of fat portions from some of the firstborn of his flock, and God looked upon him with favor. Whereas, Cain didn't receive favor for his offerings and became angry with God. Scripture goes on to tell us that God admonished Cain to do right, for in so doing He too would receive favor. Now here's that divergent reference that God made, not only for Cain, but for all of humanity – "If you do what is right, will you not be accepted? But if you do not do what is right, sin is crouching at your door; it desires to have you, but you must rule over it."

Saints, just in case you don't know it, arrogance or pride as we also know it to be, is a sin before God. The Bible instructs us to be mindful of the fact that pride comes before the fall – of course you know the rest of the story how Cain lured Abel into the fields and killed him. If only Cain had humbled himself unto God as his brother did, there is no way of knowing just how bountiful God may have blessed him. But instead, Cain was cursed by God, telling him that the ground that he worked would no longer yield him any crops – telling Cain that he would from now on be a restless wanderer on the earth. What an awful fate that didn't have to be. As for you and I, a two-fold gift is what we can offer unto God while life has us on stand-by: at all times, remain humble – and even when you have not attained the level of success that you desire, work with what you have and give God your very best.

I cannot emphasize enough the importance of having a good or right attitude, particularly while God is working things out for your life. And anyway, nobody wants to be bothered with some arrogant, rude, un-grateful, selfish, self-centered, bitter person that constantly complains about what they don't have, but never showing any gratitude or appreciation for the things that they do have – at least I know for sure that I don't want to be bothered by it. Can you imagine that God feels exactly the same way? Take for instance, in Exodus 14:21, where the Jews that were enslaved by the Egyptians – and after Moses had done what God commanded him to do by telling Pharaoh to let his people go – you would think that there would be a deep seated sense of gratitude to God for what He had caused to happen on their behalf. Hardly – even after Moses took his staff and commanded the Red Sea to open, giving them safe passage from Pharaoh and his vicious army, clearly their hearts were not filled to the brim with gratitude, because like true church folk, the Bible tells us that they wandered in the desert for forty years, when in reality, they could have made it to the promised land in eleven days – angry with Moses, angry with God, all the while taking their eyes off of God, and directing their focus on their own selfish, prideful, sin-directed behavior as they opted for creating graven images, as they wandered aimlessly and needlessly for forty years. The take away from this story is that while on stand-by, while we patiently wait in the meantime, we need to incorporate the right attitude in our spirit – always be in position to hear from God and be prepared to govern ourselves accordingly. I know first-hand that sometimes while in stand-by mode, it seems as if God hasn't heard your prayers; sometimes it appears that God's timing is all wrong; sometimes you may have thought that God has forgotten about you. But saints, let me assure you that as that old gospel song reminds us, "He may not come when you want Him, but He's always on time." Only God knows your perfect timing for every season of your life. Here is what one of His Minor Prophets by the name of Habakkuk says in a major way about what is to come in your life as you move through your stand-by season of success – Habakkuk 2:3 – "For the vision is yet for the appointed time, but at the end it shall speak and not lie. Though it tarry, wait for it, because it will surely come to pass." NLT. True success can be found in the stand-by lanes that God places us.

Devotional

All of my life, I have been told that patience is a virtue; at least that's what the elders implored. Paul, as he referenced the church at Galatia, insisted that patience is "one of the fruits of the Spirit. Wow, here it is suggested by Paul, that patience has such great significance and yet, so many Christians today frown on the very idea of having to be patient – for so many, waiting on anything is not an option; it's not even on their microwave ready radar. But for those that understand the blessings in waiting on God to move on your behalf, you have been deemed as virtuous. It echoes your conviction that, even though you are going through a storm, you know a man that can speak to the wind and the rain and make them behave; you are the ones that understand that while the enemy tries to block your attempts to succeed, God will step in and make them your footstool; yes, you my dear family, are the ones that know without a doubt, that while you travail through the valley of the shadow of death – you understand that the shadow is bigger than the problem or the event, and while the valley may be dark, there is a bright side on the other side of through – and you patiently endured to the end to tell Him, thank you for being there as you valiantly persevered to your breakthrough.

Prayer

I've come to understand and embrace the fact that there is a time and place for everything and everybody. This is just a fact of life that we all are subjected to, and ultimately, there isn't much we can do about it. Anxiety and frustrations are commonplace for persons who are determined to not allow their current situation or season of lack define who they are and will subsequently become. But the Bible tells us to, "be anxious for nothing..." Philippians 4: 4 – 7 (NLT); and therefore, Oh, God, I pray for peace and calm for those who may have grown anxious as they impatiently pursue their dreams and goals of success. I pray, Father, that Your peace that surpasses all understanding will enter into their hearts and minds, shall prevail as you work on their behalf. This is your servant's prayer, in the name of Jesus, amen.

CHAPTER SEVEN

Stay in Your Assigned Seat (A Tailor Made Destiny)

One size fits all is not the way God designed humanity – no two of us are exactly the same. I can remember when I first learned that our God is so incredibly awesome, that He is able to design an individual snowflake so uniquely different, that no other snowflake is identical to the next. Yes, our God is the Master Designer of all designers. And furthermore, no two sets of fingerprints are identical, and most certainly, no two paths to success are the same. Along life's highway, many may be on the same road, and yet, experience uniquely different trials and tribulations, even though their aims may bear similarities.

With God, proper placement is everything – God has carefully crafted specific things, places, opportunities, and outcomes, that will have far reaching implications guaranteeing you the success that you so desire. However, if you are out of place, you interrupt the divine process that was tailor made just for you. I cannot express to you with enough passion and concern, just how frustrated I get when I travel by air, and I'm brought to a screeching halt while headed to my assigned seat, because someone is sitting in somebody else's seat; somebody is out of place – oh, the frustration that it causes me. Occasionally, and rarely, does this problem get resolved by the passengers, but more often than not, it requires the assistance of the flight attendant – and of course, by then, I, along with several other passengers have been irritated before we even take off.

Preparing to take-off towards your goal of success in life can often cause confusion and irritation not only to yourself, but others as well, if you're not careful. And remaining focused and anchored on your goals is paramount to determining whether you fail or succeed. Too often, we don't pay attention to the details of the plan and this can cause us to take our eyes away from the fine print – the small things that can trip us up and get us out of position. I'm sure that if the air traveler that incorrectly props his or her rear-end in the wrong seat had only paid attention to the details on the printed ticket, they would have realized that there is a difference between a window seat and an aisle seat; the letters B and D are similar, but if you look close enough you can glean the distinction; the letters E and F, can also trip you up if you're glancing rather than focusing on the details.

I used those illustrations to make this point – God is intentional, God doesn't make mistakes and He knows the paths that are assigned to each our lives. And God requires us to pay close attention to the details that are meant to be prescriptive for each of us to follow. Yes, mistakes can and will happen on our part; there will be times when we will slip up and deviate from God's plan. However, for those who are content and determined with becoming professional seat jumpers – you know the ones, the ones that are more apt to look over at your situation and determine that the grass is greener on your side of the street. Those are the ones that don't realize that things are not as they always appear – they are not aware that just because the grass is greener, doesn't mean that it is better – because beautiful grass has been known to grow very lush and green over a cesspool.

Those professional seat jumpers tend not to understand or care about what you had to go through to get to where you are in life – they operate under the assumption that if they do what you did, perhaps they can create a short-cut to the goal line of success. Again, God is intentional – what is for you, is for you – and what is for me, is for me. Your skillset and equipping are what you acquired along the way to better prepare you for the road ahead. Your lived experiences, all of them, are what contributed to your shaping and molding according to God's prescription for the end product, called, YOU! And regardless as to what other folk may think, what worked for you, more than likely will not work for them. This is why it is important for us to understand the significance of getting in our own seat so that God can work on us in a place that is tailor made to bless us – God desires to shape us and mold us and make us into something special and unique – something that no one else could have done but God.

When I read the newspapers and watch television, I'm always entranced by the various singing, talent shows, such as the Voice, So You Think You Can Sing, American Idol, America's Got Talent, and the likes – and I am always at a loss for words when I see how many and different talented people there are in the world. I sometimes find myself scratching my head in wonderment, because it seems like there is this never-ending flow of gifted and talented people, who come from as many and varied backgrounds with an equal amount of distinctly different personal experiences, and yet they find themselves at the same place in life – performing on an international stage, attempting to successfully accomplish the very same thing, sharing the same aim and yet, operating from their own prescriptive, assigned, seat that God has intentionally prepared, solely and uniquely for each of them – this my brothers and sisters is what God wants to do for all of us.

Finally, I get excited when I'm reminded that God has what I like to think of as the "Buddy System. "Whenever we can't, God can. Whenever we won't, God will. Whenever we don't, God does. But, God, in all of

His Omniscience, even after promising in the 23rd division of Psalm, as He declares, that He will be with us even until the end of the earth, God does not impose His will upon us – God prefers that we take the gift of free-will and follow His plans for each of our lives – all He is saying then, is that we get in our assigned seats, buckle-up and enjoy the flight – because He is prepared to take up to places we've never been, do things we've never done, and see things we've never seen – Get in your assigned seat!

Devotional

In the movie, Changing Lanes, Samuel L. Jackson's character and Ben Affleck's character collided on the interstate, mainly due to the fact that they each were preoccupied with personal matters, rather than being focused on the highway. And needlessly to say, this fateful collision set a series of frustrations and problems in motion than neither of the two could have imagined in a lifetime. Their lives were literally turned upside down and the impact of them being thrust out of their required lanes of relative safety, negatively touched every area of their lives. From a ministry perspective, I can honestly say that I cannot begin to remember how many times church mess originated from somebody (s) who intentionally got into someone else's lane, or as is commonly referred to, as their business. Being concerned and involved where you need not be has become inherently problematic for those that are seeking clarity and resolve concerning the matter of overcoming life's pitfalls and obstacles, as they persevere and press towards successfully fulfilling their dreams. Several Scriptures come to mind whenever I reflect on the mindless antics of some church folk in particular. Initially, I think that if people would remember what Psalm 119: 105 – 108 says – "Your word is a lamp for my feet and a light for my path. I've promised it once, and I'll promise it again: I will obey your wonderful laws. I have suffered much,

O Lord; restore my life again, just as you promised. Lord, accept my grateful thanks and teach me your laws." (NLT). I think this particular text is as good a place as any to assist with clarifying how important it is to see that God knows exactly what He's doing as He leads and guides us through and to our destiny. First of all, this text is personal; David's utterances indicate he is acutely aware of what happens when he gets out of his lane and does things his way – he knows that it is a sin. But he's also pleading unto God his case, as he reminds God that he is still capable of keeping his promise a second time, even though he flunked the test the first time. When was the last time you found yourself promising God you'll do better next time, and sincerely mean it? The bottom line is that God has established a lamp and a light to guide us through toils and snares of our own, and we don't need to be in someone else's lane creating un-necessary havoc that has nothing to do with God and His plans for our lives – just stay in your lane; the one that God designed specifically and perfectly for you.

Prayer

Eternal, and Everlasting, God – today I surrender my whole self, unto you. I ask that wherever you desire me to go, I will follow. And in so doing, Dear Lord, cause me to walk down the path prepared just for me, and please release me from the temptation to encroach on anyone else's path, so that I may not interfere with your plans of success for their lives. This is my prayer, in Jesus' name, amen.

CHAPTER EIGHT

Letting Go of the Throttle (Controls)

I often wonder if anyone other than me remember the popular bumper-sticker slogan that read – "Jesus is my co-pilot." If you did, I hope you rejected that mantra as I did; that is patently, bad theology! To suggest that Jesus is the co-pilot, puts us in the driver's seat – and with God, nothing could be further from the truth. Actually, we can count it a blessing just to be onboard. In-spite of what some may believe, God is still in control – He orders our steps, He determines our destiny, He makes a way out of no way – God, throughout all of time, remains in control.

Admittedly there are times when we are tempted to think that we are in control, taking matters into our own hands, and sometimes we get in God's way and attempt to take hold of the throttle of life while steering in the wrong direction and headed down the wrong runways that occasionally end in self-destruction, and potentially resulting in missing the mark for success. But God has already declared His authority to all of humanity when in Hebrews 12:2, James says, "Jesus is the author and finisher of our faith." NLT. The problematic here is that after having successfully matriculated through various institutions of higher learning, earning Bachelors and Masters degrees and beyond, we often find ourselves attempting to rely on our own knowledge and expertise rather than letting God show us who, what, when, where, and how to discover and enjoy that thing that we call success.

When God orders our steps, there are no statute of limitations on our dreams for success – I think that warrants a pause for a praise break – Hallelujah!!!!! Just think, through it all, after everything we've attempted to accomplish, and didn't get it right, God was still there, picking up the pieces, while operating in His divine power, cleaning up our mess and fixing the broken things in and of our lives – trust me, it is always in His hands – He is always in control. I cannot begin to imagine where I would be had God not intervened on my behalf and snatched me from the grip of chaos, miss-information, and misdirection. Just to think about all of the potential negative and destructive outcomes that I could have claimed ownership, still after many years, gives me the creeps, literally. It would really serve us well to at all times remember that everything about us, is always in God's hands – He is still in control.

And what better place is there to be, than in God's hands? I'm sure that if we were to inquire of Job, how did he feel and how did he know that beyond the boundaries of his trials, disappointments and challenges, that God would yet bring him through it all, he would tell us that, all God did was to ask Satan to consider him – but the caveat was that Satan could not harm or destroy him. Job would probably tell us that it was then that he knew that he would be victorious (successful) because of his faith and trust in God. Of course, both you and I know that Job, much like us, was not thrilled about the hardship of losing his children, wife, friends, cattle, community standing, and wealth, but where Job shines is through his unyielding faith – "though you slay me, yet will I trust you!" And because Job proved to God that he could be trusted – God blessed him with double what he took from him – Job, by any stretch of the imagination, was successful because he allowed his everything, including himself, to remain in God's hands, under the power and authority of God's control!

For many of us, we are on a regular basis, so strongly tempted to want to be in control; sometimes we even feel a sense of worthlessness if we're not in the driver's seat. Life, according to how God operates, has to sometimes drive us. We don't always need to know where God is taking us; we won't always feel comfortable with how God is getting us there; we may not even know why God is yet desirous of taking us anywhere, when we take into account the countless times that we disobeyed Him, the many times that we slapped His hands, while turning a blind eye and deaf ear to His directives.

I've found that even after the Master has leveled us to the ground, many yet remain un-fazed and un-humbled by His power and control over our lives and situations. My own personal experiences have resulted in finding myself in a stupor of fear of sorts. Now I ask myself, how can I lie to God, saying I trust you, God, and yet hold on to this fear that I carry on my shoulders and within my heart? Finally, it dawned on me, that every time that I felt myself being afraid of not being in control, it had everything, and I do mean everything to do with the fact that I couldn't see way down the road far enough to give me the confidence to let go of the controls.

I came to terms with the fact that I was walking by sight and not by faith. And it happens to the very best of us. It is however, unfortunate, because as Christians, as believers, all we really need to do is to play back in our mind's eye and recall all that God had already done in our lives and for our good, and having never seen Him, sooner than later we should be able to cross over and relinquish the controls over to Him.

That great idea that He gave you; the operative is, He gave it to you – whether in a dream, while meditating, or perhaps it was birthed from a deep conversation with a colleague – the operative is that He gave it to you. That burning passion inside your soul to be a successful entrepreneur, lawyer, teacher, community activist, politician, scientist, or even an author – God gave that to you through His D.N.A. – Divine Nurturing of the Almighty; by design, it's in your bones, piercing your heart, occupying your every thought – the operative is, He gave it to you. And when God gives you something, He wants us to make full proof of it, but He still retains ownership, thereby retaining control over it and you; Scripture tells us that God declared that the earth is His and the fullness thereof – He is in full control.

I surmise that this particular chapter will perhaps be the most challenging for you to adjust your feelings and clearly see yourself as you really need to be seen when it comes to letting go and letting God take control. And there should be no shame to your game, because this is certainly something that has either already plagued many a dreamer, or continues to do so, even now. My own personal account of not fully trusting God enough to relinquish control over to Him, is nothing short of laughable.

The fear of letting go can be problematic because it requires that we get on board with God's plans for our lives, while fully relying on Him as we are rendered as passengers of our own journey down the road to success. Everybody has a story or two in them that reflects moments when they didn't fully trust God in spite of what their mouths were saying; everybody at one time or another has felt the angst of the feeling of not being in control. It is a given that we share a common thread when it comes down to saying what we believe about putting it all in His hands and what we actually do about it. I thought I would treat you to some of my close friends' perspectives on the matter of feeling being not in control and what it does to you when you believe that you're helpless and powerless to determine any outcome – their voices, in their own words, can be read at the end of this chapter.

By now, however, I hope that you have felt compelled to do some kind of personal inventory about what does your faith look like when it comes to trusting God with your life and your dreams. Self-introspection can be vitally important for anyone that is committed to the task of doing the extraordinary. However, breaking out of the shell of mediocrity sometimes seems impossible, mainly because many of us get too comfortable with doing as little as possible while desiring for big things to take place.

The Bible admonishes us about attempting to take matters into our own hands. Proverbs 3:5 says, "Trust in the Lord with all your heart, and do not lean on your own understanding." NLT. For those of you who may be chiseling away at trying to do things your way without first talking to God and then to no avail, let me encourage you to join me as we peek in on what is going on in Proverbs 3:5. First of all, the book of Proverbs tells us about people who have wisdom and enjoy its benefits. There are three tenets in this book that I would like to lift and share with you that I believe will have long-range benefits for you as you press forward towards becoming successful in life.

Here are the three that I have selected for your blessing, and they are: trust in the Lord, put God first, and listen to learn. First, let us examine the trust factor – who else can you go to that can do more for you than God? I venture to say, however, that a far too many that pray to God for a breakthrough or a miracle, often go to everybody else prior to taking it to God in prayer; and that everybody else rarely has your best interest at heart. But God's word can be trusted and tested – He cannot lie or fail. But your so-called friends on the other hand, sometimes are jealous of you being so trusting and bold in your relationship with God, and oftentimes, they desire to have that same dream and drive for success that you possess, but t are unwilling to do what God asks of them – and that is to just trust Him.

You cannot trump God's plans for your life if He is determined that they are to come to pass! And your faith and trust in Him are the cornerstone beliefs that provides you with the courage and conviction to do so. You must ask yourself whether or not you really believe in God, or is it just street corner lip service? The blessing in trusting God, is that when you let go and let God – the Concealed God, now becomes the Revealed

God. In other words, God, then shows up in miraculous and wondrous ways in your life once you have relinquished the reigns unto Him – once you have let go of the throttle. Will you be anxious? If you are human you surely just might be. However, the Bible tells us to be anxious for nothing – so then, I encourage you to opt out of being anxious and opt into being excited and expectant. Yes, for the believer, getting excited about what all is to come on your behalf; and being expectant about the plans He has for your success should bring you great joy – knowing that no one can beat God's giving.

Earlier I mentioned that part of the problem with many as it pertains to letting go, is that some folk go to everybody else first and after they have exhausted their running to and fro, they come to the altar and place it all there. Summarily, this is so wrong in so many ways. God desires a more intense trust from us – He desires that our trust would be borne out of a deep seated love for who He is and what He has already demonstrated according to His Omniscience. I could only imagine that God might perceive us to be just a bit more spiritually quirky than He anticipated – let's see; He gave your life; He gave you a purpose; He gave you a dream; He gave you passion; He gave you providence, and yet, you seek one another for the answers to being successful – God simply wants you to Fully Rely On Him – If you really trust God, then take it to God in prayer, first and foremost.

Finally, you must be willing to yield to the sound of God's voice and His activities. You must be quiet when God is speaking. The Bible tells us in Psalm 46:10 – "Be silent, and know that I am God!" NLT. Oh, what a privilege it is to be able to hear from God. Perhaps one of the greatest mistakes for a believer to make, is to tune the world in, and tune God out. Sometimes, God comes in the form of a midnight whisper in the solitude of your darkness. And then, other times God appears as a jubilant song of praise and worship as a choir and congregation sing His praises of deliverance, of healing, of miracles, of signs and wonders – and even in the midst of it all –the calamity of joy is still a silent one, because God is speaking, God is still working things out, God is still teaching – listen and learn. God is still thinking that thing through, He's still working it out just for you – Although it may seem that nothing is working for your good, simply because you're not controlling things, don't panic and don't give in to fear – God is still in control!

Devotional

There is something interesting about the common thread that runs through all of humanity. Think about it – why is it that, no matter who you are, where you come from or what station you are in life, we all have this "control" issue. I mean, there's something to be said about us wanting to hold the throttle of life and never wanting to let go of it. Even when it becomes clear that, after a few futile attempts, we not only don't know where we're going, but we remain clueless as to how to get there – amazing, utterly amazing behavior. However, that's just the way it is, so much so that it is reflected in in spiritual walk – God says, "Go right," and we are determined to go left. Just to keep it simple right here – if God's thoughts are not our thoughts and His ways are not our ways, at what point do we cease and desist with the foolishness of being obstinate and disobedient, and begin to obey God? I've discovered that, as the Author and Finisher of our faith, God not only knows where we're going, but He also knows how to get us there, and in one piece I might add – I don't know about you, but I'm letting go of the throttle and letting God handle His business – I trust that you will come to know that whatever it is that you're struggling with, whatever it is that you might be in need of, don't you attempt to go at it alone, – let it go, God's got this!

Prayer

God give me the strength and the fortitude that I need to remain steadfast, and full of faith, as I attempt to relinquish control of the throttle of life – make yourself known in my fears and impose your presence and will, on my bouts of darkness that are sometimes shrouded in the uncertainty of what tomorrow might bring. Today, God, show up and take control of my destiny as I press towards my goals for success – this is my humble prayer, in Jesus' name, amen.

CHAPTER NINE

Beware of Spiritual Terrorists

"The church is the only institution that kills its wounded."

–DR. MARK LOMAX, PROFESSOR OF HOMILETICS,
THE INTERDENOMINATIONAL THEOLOGICAL CENTER,
ATLANTA, GEORGIA – 2005

One of the most disturbing and tragic realities known to the Christian faith, is the fact that oftentimes, there are countless worshipers in our midst on Sunday mornings, that have hopes and dreams of one day, sooner than later, of ceasing to live below their blessing threshold – in other words, they have plans to have a better life; they've made up their minds that success is within their reach. But, unfortunately, they have people in their lives that are either, jealous, envious, spiteful or just plain hateful and mean – so much so, that they've become spiritually and sometimes physically toxic and occasionally, deadly – these are the Spiritual Terrorists among us.

Everybody in church, at one time or another, has either been through something, is now going through something, or at the very least, one day, will most certainly go through something that will bring them to the tipping point of life – that place where they either believe that they can't go on any further, or they can decree that they can do all things through Christ which strengthens them – meaning that the enemy thought he had them, but by the grace, and un-merited favor of God, they made it anyway.

But, conversely, there will always be an ever presence of evil – the spiritual terrorists that will come to kill your hopes and dreams, regardless of who you are. And, to my amazement, not only are they in the church, but they are prospering through generational foolishness on Holy Ground. There was a time in our churches when Testimonial Sunday was considered to be breakthrough Sunday. This was the time in the worship experience someone that perhaps had been through the fire, had suddenly found themselves not only having been brought out of the fire, but was ready and willing to tell the other saints of God about had it not been for the Lord on their side...

People used to look forward to hearing about the awesome ways God was working in someone else's behalf; there used to be a certain kind of excitement that permeated the atmosphere that would bring about loud utterances of praise and gratitude unto God for having done the un-imagined impossible; church folk used to live and die by the testimony of others, that declared that God ain't dead and nor is He done with us just yet.

But a strange and sad thing has happened in too many of our churches – the devil has found a roosting place; he has multiplied and clothed his imps in many different titles, positions and garments. Now a days, a person cannot comfortably come and stand in front of the church and talk about the goodness of God without having their testimony twisted and trampled upon by some jealous and envious spiritual terrorist. And by all accounts, the church was once the one place that was determined safe and loving enough to openly share our hurts, our pains, our disappointments, as well as our hopes and dreams of overcoming the odds and succeeding at what we had set our sights on – Beware of the spiritual terrorists!

It's a sad day when it has become almost taboo to enter into His gates with thanksgiving, only to have someone crouching and waiting to pounce on your testimony; waiting to steal your joy. It appears that Joseph's Biblical story about dealing with jealous and envious brothers is alive and well in the 21st century church. As you may recall, Joseph was just a little too talkative about his dreams and plans, and ultimately, after aborting plans to kill him, his brothers sold him off into slavery – they were by all accounts, spiritual terrorists, determined to break his hopeful spirit – imagine that, his own flesh and blood.

Familial terrorizing is in fact a reality in many of our families. However, as sad and ridiculous as it is, it should come as no surprise that everybody that pats you on the back and cheer you on, truthfully, are not sincere and genuine with their gestures of well wishing, even though they are blood kin. As for me, though, I have come to respond to my spirit of discernment rather attentively, and can pick them out of a crowd almost blind folded.

Sibling rivalry is something that humankind inherited since the beginning of time. I've always winced in silence whenever I hear someone say that, blood is thicker than water. Perhaps in most accounts there's a pound of truth to it, but from Scripture to the bloody streets of our culture, blood has and continues to lose out to water; families are killing each other at an alarming, un-explainable rate that seemingly shares no logic. And to a great extent, I suppose that much of the heartless carnage comes from the family – but the blood that is supposed to bind has loosened its grip.

A few years ago, I heard from a very close friend of mine. One day out of the blue he called me on the phone to tell me that, a dear cousin, one of whom he had respected to the utmost; telling me that he had approached his cousin about investing in an up-start record label that he had high expectations. Well, it seems that his cousin, acting in what he thought would be a confidential gesture to a mutual family friend, remarked that he thought that my friend was a shyster. Needlessly to say, my friend was confused and distraught, because he and his cousin had never shared a cross word or bad feelings between them.

Well, apparently the spirit of jealously and envy had been a part of his cousin's spirit for quite a while. But what my friend couldn't come to terms with, is the fact that his cousin had everything. He had a very lucrative career, a big fancy house, fine, expensive cars, a loving wife and daughter, but yet, he didn't hesitate to try and undermine my friend's dreams of becoming successful in the music industry – and to this day, he still shakes his head at the thought that his own flesh and blood turned out to be a spiritual terrorist – sometimes family can turn out to be your own worst enemy – beware of spiritual terrorists in your own bloodline.

As a pastor, one of the biggest misconceptions that I've had to address with many of my congregants as they would sit in my study and share with me their stories of how they were deceived and betrayed by other church members is literally astounding. You would think that the church would be a safe harbor to come and share the joys and sorrows of your Christian journey. However, and sadly, in many instances, that's just not the case. I've heard stories of how after someone had given a testimony about the goodness of the Lord and how He had miraculously moved on their behalf, and one of their best friends had sat on the same pew, would gossip and lie, while the member was up giving their testimony.

I'm determined to be honest and transparent with any and everybody. But, unfortunately, some people just can't handle the truth – do I put a lot of time and effort with intentional prayer for you and your family's life, love, and success? Yes, of course I do – but I'm also charged with the responsibility to always tell you the truth. And the truth is that, not always will church folk like you, or the stories about your great life and your hopes and dreams of success. Now that may hurt you right about now – but it is the truth. You have to be ever mindful that the devil goes to church too. And the devil is not interested in your good relationship with God; all the devil wants to do is to steal, kill and destroy, each and every dream of success that you can muster; all he wants to do is to steal you from God; all he wants to do is to kill your spiritual appetite to push forward towards your dreams of succeeding; all he wants to do is to deny you your dreams. And, as Christians we must be on guard, we must be vigilant and we must be discerning – and we must be aware of the fact that, just because someone is in church, does not necessarily mean that they have church in them – some church goers only show up to terrorize other church goers – sisters and brothers, don't you be fooled by smiling faces and pats on the back – beware of church going spiritual terrorist because they are real.

Some of the worst terrorizing comes from the highest perches of denominationalism. In the book of Genesis 1: 26 – 28, the word of God says, "Let Us make man in Our image, according to Our likeness; let them have dominion over the fish of the sea, over the birds of the air, and over the cattle, over all the earth and over every creeping thing that creeps on the earth." 27 So God created man in His own image; in the image of God He created him; male and female He created them. 28 Then God blessed them, and God said to them, "Be fruitful and multiply; fill the earth and subdue it; have dominion over the fish of the sea, over the birds of the air, and over every living thing that moves on the earth." NLT.

In a post-modern church, the single most overlooked argument in this pericope, is that man has taken the word dominion and applied it across the board to include, "sovereignty over other man," or for better political correctness and inclusiveness, "humankind." This text never implies, recommends, and nor does it suggests that man is to rule over man himself. However, in many churches and various denominations we have bishops that have taken God's Holy Word and bastardize it to the point of blasphemy.

I am acutely aware of certain bishops that govern themselves as little gods; having a certain power that is designed, first to please their own terroristic mentality and spirituality and to satisfy their own lust for the world and its selfish desires. These same bishops would on many occasions apply the phrase, “Godly judgment,” to their decision making, while all along, everybody knows that many of these decisions are birthed from political motivation and personal grudges. And incredibly, their governing style and modus operandi is just what it implies; it’s downright criminal and terroristic at its core.

As I prepared to address this particular chapter, I was able to draw from an extensive pool of no less that fifty clergy and laity that harbored strong feelings and opinions about this great terroristic threat to the church, and the hopes and dreams of those that comprise the church on several levels. And for the record, I could have been able to draw from an even greater wellspring, had they not been afraid to be honest with themselves, and for fear of reprisal.

“The church is the only institution that kills its wounded!” Dr. Mark Lomax’s prophetic utterance back in 2005, still resonates throughout the halls of religion. The question must be asked, then, what good is leadership in the church, if it is determined to abdicate godly-leadership and focus its energies and sights on money grubbing, church politics and self-promotion, while there are those that follow said leadership with hopes and dreams of becoming better Christians and servant leaders themselves?

What is to become of the dreams of the many followers of these bishops that constantly find themselves belittled, bullied, and beaten down, both emotionally and spiritually by these spiritual terrorists? In my various conversations with clergy and laity, it was determined that so many had and still have gifts, talents, and missions of success in life that have gone by the way of doubt and fear, and sometimes spiritual blindness – in other words, they find themselves following a personality rather than following after Christ. I’m known for telling people that church folk are more afraid of the devil than they are of God. And of course, they want to know how I arrived at that conclusion – and I gently remind them that if they feared God more, we wouldn't have as much hell in our churches as we do, starting from the top down. I tell them that if they feared God more, they would not let someone who puts their pants or skirts on the same as the next person have the kind of dominion over their lives that for the most part, yields nothing worthwhile of long lasting relevance.

Spiritual terrorists are not just in our churches, but they are there thriving much to the dismay of God. I believe that Christ is immensely disappointed. I believe that Jesus is still waiting on a great many of us to take Him at His word when He declared, "I came that you may have life and have it more abundantly." NLT. I believe that when the "real" body of Christ rises up and fully trust and rely on God, much of the ecclesiastical foolishness will cease to exist and those that dare to dream, those that desire to become better, and those that are determined to succeed according to God's portion and passion, will in fact become who God intended them to be, realizing that what God has for you, is for you, and no demon in hell shall prevail against what God has established – Beware of spiritual terrorists, – your success hinges on it!

Devotional

Instilling fear into someone, automatically makes you a bully with terroristic tendencies. Tendencies, that are apt to manifest over time, because many of us allow it to happen. But as believers of the gospel of Jesus Christ, we are admonished just like Paul admonished Timothy, to paraphrase, we don't own fear and fear doesn't own us – there will be occasional visitations by fear, but we have the power and authority to dismiss fear and send it back to hell, from whence it came. The time, energy and resources that we pour into fear is an absolute waste, and sin before God; and we regularly miss our deliverance and breakthroughs because we are afraid that someone over us will take exception to our conviction and tenacity to assert ourselves and fear God more than the devil and his imps. Today, tell the devil to go straight to hell; tell him that there is nothing about him that can scare you any longer; tell the devil that the same God that kicked him out of heaven, can and will continue to reign victorious over earth, and all that is in it, including him – go ahead, I dare you – and if you do, You Win – "greater is He that is in me, than he that is in the world.) 1 John 4:4 (NIV).

Prayer

Dear God, I know of your strength and your might, and I reverence you. I ask that you continue to put a hedge of protection around me, my family and my friends. And God, as difficult as it may seem sometimes, I ask that you bless even my enemies, the spiritual terrorists that are running rampant, because I realize that they need you, too. Father, give me the strength and conviction to continually renounce the devil and his attempts to separate me from You – give me the power to flex my spiritual muscles to put him behind me and under my feet forever more – in the Mighty, Matchless, name of Jesus, I pray, amen.

CHAPTER TEN

Stick With the Flight Plan

Many of us go through life with every step, twist and turn already planned out. The road map and obstacle courses of life have been identified and a desired successful strategy has been established and initiated. But one day we wake up and realize that the plans that we had for our self, and the place where we purposed our life to take root and have meaning, looks nothing like our master plan. Today, if I may, I'd like to encourage and help somebody along the way, by reminding you that, if God is not in the plan, then you have the wrong plan. God, our Father in heaven, has a purpose, a plan, and a place for each of us to flourish, and it's a place called, Over There. Your place may not look like mine, nor mine like yours. But, if we listen to God when He tells us to go Over There, then I can assure you that God has already taken care of the necessary details to properly guide, protect, and provide for you. When God says, go Over There, just go! Follow His Master Plan – there's a blessing in it for you, I promise – Stick with the Flight Plan.

Changing plans can and will present challenges and frustrations, merely because we've grown accustomed to thinking and believing that the first draft rendered is the final document that describes our flight path to our destiny. God is the Author and Finisher of our faith and our respective destinies. But what presents itself as a challenge for some, is the matter of taking our eyes off of God – the Bible admonishes that obedience is better than sacrifice – and in this case, it simply means that if we intend to become all that God has designed us to be, it becomes more of an acute matter of doing what God told us to do – stick with the flight plan.

While it may not appear that what God is telling us to do makes sense right now, it is, however, important to note that, His thoughts are not our thoughts, and His ways are not our ways – God knows all, and He sees all. After all, God knows what's best for our life – He created us for success; He created us to be fruitful and to multiply. God created us with gifts and passions that speak to positive outcomes that blesses not only us, but others as well. Yes, there is a flight plan for our lives, a plan that can take you higher than you've ever been, a plan that will introduce you to people that you only dreamed of meeting, a plan that will take you to places and shores that on your own, you would never have been able to travel – God is telling each of us to stick with the flight plan.

In this wonderful and sometimes overwhelming 21st century technological age that we now live, we can enjoy a life that our forefathers and foremothers could never have imagined. And one of the most amazing inventions is the automobile navigation system. Our cars are now equipped with technology that can guide and direct us to our destinations with just a minimum amount of input from us – put in the address and the navigation system can take you from New York to Los Angeles, and all we need to do is follow the directions.

The same applies to the technology of our cell phones; our phones are now more of everything else, than just a phone call away – on our phones we can now search the World Wide Web; discovering facts and un-earthing information that the old Encyclopedia Britannica could provide. Just like the navigation system in our automobiles, our phones can also guide and direct us to our desired destinations. But I am most amazed with the technology that is built into the design of our airplanes – once the pilot initiates inputting the flight data into the plane's computer, the entire flight plan is established from take-off to landing. However, what I really find truly amazing, is that should the pilot desires, he can put the plane on auto-pilot, and the plane can literally fly itself, solely because it operates on the flight plan that the pilot initiated. If there is turbulence, the plane knows how to react; if there's a fuel problem, the plane knows what to do; if there is inclement weather, the plane knows what to do; if there is an emergency, the plane knows to alert the pilot and afterwards, on command, it relinquishes control over to the one that is in charge.

Don't you find it amazing that here is a good illustration as to how God has designed our flight plan? I believe that much like how a pilot loads a plane's computer with all of the necessary flight data that it needs to fly itself, God, in the same way, does that exact same thing with each of us through His DNA – Divine Nurturing of the Almighty! Everything that we need in order that we may ever become the functioning, living, soaring, human organism that God intended, is imbedded in us upon arrival. In other words, when we get here, we are already equipped with more than we really need to do what thus says the Lord – God designed us to come into this world with the potential to succeed above and beyond our wildest expectations – God made us in a way that causes us to know that, yes, we can do all things through Christ Jesus, which gives us our strength.

And I'm excited about the very thought of me being able to do all things through my, Lord and Savior, Jesus Christ! Therefore, I'm convinced that whatever I set my mind to, I can achieve it; I can rise above the doubts and fears that haunt me day and night, and claim victory through success, with God being my Helper; I can make it through the turbulence and storms of life and not be defeated, denied or destroyed; I can endure the roughest sides of the mountain and not be afraid to climb; I can run and not grow weary and I can walk and not faint. And the same applies to you. We are all fearfully and wonderfully made in God's image, with His characteristics and make-up – we possess the power and the wherewithal to succeed if we only stick with the flight plan – yes, there are inventions to be invented, there are businesses to be created, books to be written and dreams to be fulfilled – Stick with the flight plan.

I can remember so vividly when God spoke my name and called me into the ministry. I didn't want to hear it; I refused to allow myself to be taken away from the path and plans that I had established for my life. Now please don't get it twisted – I felt God's prodding and I could clearly hear His voice, but I was caught in a holding pattern that was very comfortable and complimentary to what I wanted for my life. I had seen enough of what goes on in certain churches, and I must admit that I had become jaded at how ministry was being done. My plan was to do everything that opposed the religiosity of the day.

For instance, I just couldn't see myself pastoring a flock that was insistent on behaving more like goats than sheep. It didn't make sense – and later on in life after I gave in to God and began my pastorate, I would from time to time remind certain folk, that I'm a shepherd and not a goat herder. In my opinion, too many church goers were continuously coming to church for all the wrong reasons – church is not a social club; it's neither a fraternity nor sorority; church is not a place to be entertained. But rather, church out to be the one place where you can come and experience an encounter with Christ; church out to be the one place where miracles can manifest and deliverance and transformation can take place. And since I never saw any of those things transpire on the regular, I simply stayed in my lane as I continued to tell God no.

Funny thing about God – you can run but you cannot hide. When God plucks you out of the miry clay of your own plans and your own self-induced mess, for the sole purpose of using you for kingdom work, there ain't nothing you can do about it; no, nothing at all, except eventually give in to His will and His plans for your life. It took me approximately eighteen years of running from God before I finally said yes. For eighteen years of my life I tried everything humanly possible to have it my way; trying to the best of my ability to live out my life according to my plans – and what I grew to really love and appreciate about God, is that through it all, He covered, protected and provided for me above and around every mistake, every misstep – and yes, there were many. But the greatest thing that occurred as I grew weak from running and tired from screaming no – God was right there waiting when I breathed out the words, I give, have your way in my life, God – make your plans, my plans, because I trust you with my whole heart and all of my soul. God heard me on that day – and following God's plans for my life has led me to some people, places, and things, that I don't room enough, nor the time to expound, but through all of it, His grace has proven time and time again, to be more than sufficient – I know beyond a shadow of a doubt that He desires to bless each of us beyond measure, but we must be willing to stick with His plans – for He will never leave us, nor will He forsake us, He will be with us, even until the end of time – stick with the flight plan.

Devotional

20/20 faith, believe it or not, is what a lot of so-called Christians possess. I know that this is perhaps a bitter pill to swallow, but as a pastor, I can attest to the validity of that statement. Which always gives credence to the adage: "we walk by sight, and not by faith." In other words, many have been tested and continue to be tested on their faith, daily. Seriously, what good does it do for you to come to the altar Sunday after Sunday, with the same petition to God? If you really don't trust Him, then why bother? God has already told each of us that He knows what plans that He has for our lives, and yet, so many of us, take that little bit of education that we have and begin to try and out think God. Here's a confession for you – I was one of those persons once upon a time; and God let me go right ahead and self-destruct, only to bring my back at His feet. Beloved, there is not a thought that we've had, that God has not already thought out. There's not a plan devised, that God has not already perfected. There's not an outcome that God has not prepared and provided for – God knows all and sees all; His thoughts are not our thoughts and His ways are not our ways – and it's designed that way in order that we may come under His submission and follow His plans.

Prayer

Lead me, guide me, keep me from all hurt, harm and danger; cover me and shelter me, Oh, God, from dangers seen and un-seen. I've decided that I will follow, if You will lead – Your path for my feet has been made straight, but should I fall, or take a different direction, Father, forgive me, and come and save me from my self. I accept your sovereignty and your plans for my life. Your dominion and authority I acknowledge as Your Law for me to honor. I'm thankful that you looked passed every one of my faults, and saw the inner-workings of a sinner, saved by Your grace, that you deemed worthy enough to be loved by you, even when others had counted me out, while some had cast me out – but, clearly, Father, You know what is best for me, and for that, wherever You go, I want to go with You ; wherever You are, I desire to be with You, and whatever plans You have for my life, I will follow, in the marvelous name of Jesus I pray, amen.

CHAPTER ELEVEN

The Best Is Yet to Come – God's Reward Program

Everybody's life experience is different. What constitutes success for one person, can take on a completely different meaning for another person. We are all informed not only by our environment, but also by our own morals and mores as well. Our beliefs and values are strong and effective determinants that impact how we view and respond to the world in which we live. And for that matter, some may think that just because they have achieved their desired goals in life, that they've now made it; they have the very best that life has to offer – in other words, for them, there's nothing left to do but enjoy the rewards of their labor. However, for others, life has had its ups and downs and crazy turn arounds. For them, life has yielded some good days and it's offered up some challenging days – but even they must admit that on more occasions than not, life has been good to them too; God has rewarded them for their faithfulness. And in the deep recesses of their hearts, they can sense that God has something better, God is working on something on their behalf that will rival anything that they've ever taken possession, something bigger and better than ever imagined.

Have you ever asked yourself the question, "things are so good for me right now, how is it possible that they could ever get any better? I don't know about you, but I've never been in a comfort zone such as that. Have I ever had some good times? Yes, God has done some awesomely, amazing things in my life – He has truly been good to me. Have I had it so good that I didn't want to be blessed with more? Absolutely not. My relationship with God has been and is now and will always be, the kind of relationship that tells me that God desires for my cup to overflow in every facet and every season of my life – God wants me and you, to never forget that He desires to love us and bless us beyond measure – and because His resources are endless and His ability is unparalleled, He can bless us any way he prefers – and if you think that you have it good right now, just stay with Him a while longer and see that the best that God has in store for you is yet to come.

The Bible, according to Isaiah 64:4 decrees that – "For since the world began, no ear has heard and no eye has seen a God like you, who works for those who wait for him!" (NLT). Not one of us can come close to being able to imagine the kind of work that God puts in as He prepares us for the next level (s) of our lives, even when we've done nothing to earn His rewards, and in spite of the fact that on more than one occasion we've failed the test and fallen down on the road to success – God has plans to trust us even the more, and reward us handsomely, because through it all, we remained faithful, though flawed, over a few things.

As a pastor, I've found that many congregants love to hear the Prophet Isaiah decree what God desires for their lives. But rarely do any of them connect the dots between God's passion for wanting to bless them and what Isaiah is emphasizing that God requires in order that they receive those bountiful blessings – yes, it's that word, "repent," again. It's as if some church folk are fearful of asking God for forgiveness and vowing to change their wayward ways. Of course, God is a conditional God – and countless people spend an inordinate amount time waiting on God to deliver on His promise to bless them real good, but all the while stalling the process with their unwillingness to repent.

I would like to encourage you right here and now to snap out of whatever is holding you back, or whatever it is that is preventing you from going to God in prayer and asking for His forgiveness – in so doing, you will be released into the divine flow of every good and perfect thing that is destined to come your way, – that was and is Isaiah's message: "forget about the former things; do not dwell on the past. See, I am doing a new thing! Now it springs u; do you not perceive it? I am making a way in the wilderness and streams in the wasteland." Isaiah 43: 18 – 19. (NIV). Saints, what an awesome reward system; your success can have everything to do with your understanding of what was just stated. Yes, perhaps like me, at one time or another, you've tried and failed at something; maybe you thought about attempting something new, but later convinced yourself that it probably wouldn't work anyway – and all of this had some bearing on your guilt of something that you'd done that God would not approve – well, according to Isaiah, God says to get over it; and I totally agree – if I may share from my own personal experiences of getting over the fear of asking God to forgive me, I simply admonish you not to go through life wasting precious time of being afraid to seek God's forgiveness – I don't know about you, but I prefer that He bless me later, rather than never – success in God is truly worth the wait, because when you do, God reward's you in ways that are difficult to wrap your brain around.

Just think about it for a moment. Remember how God rewarded you with that long awaited dream job – all because of your willingness to trust Him with your dreams and wait on it? Can you recall how life had unleashed its twists and turns on you, and you found yourself standing on the edge of a cliff, contemplating whether to jump or stand still, and

God showed up with your breakthrough and reminding you that your help can't be found in the hills, but rather, your help and your hope is in Him? God rewarded you with clarity of how He can bless you by making it clearly known, that your cry for help is anchored in desperation and dire straits, but your hope is anchored in your faith – a faith that assures you that no matter the situation, no matter the circumstance, regardless as to how things may appear, He did promise to never leave, nor forsake you. What an awesome reward to receive – just knowing that He is always there, gives us the necessary boldness to dream, and hope, and believe, and ultimately become what God ordained each of us to become: successful – in spite of our fears and the efforts and antics of others.

Being rewarded for something is a feeling that sometimes calls for wonderment. What I mean by that is that often what you are willing to do in order to receive that coveted prize just can't be explained to others. And, if I may, I will draw from many of my childhood experiences where I knew that if I did certain things according to my parents' pleasure, there was a good possibility that I would receive a reward. Take for instance, while growing up in Montgomery, Alabama during the 50s and early 60s. Payday was always grocery shopping day – if we had been good, we were permitted to go along with our parents to the grocery store. The trip alone was a major reward – but for my younger brother and I, just being able to help determine what was put in the grocery cart gave us the unexplained anxiety of anticipating that coveted prized that came with certain products.

Back in our day, Alphabet cereal and Cracker Jacks, each had a prize in the bottom of the box. And, even though it seems a little funny now, it was no laughing matter back then – we had to keep an eagle eye open to help us remember which bag the cereal and Cracker Jacks were put. Needless to say, the long ride home didn't help our anxiety level at all. Nearing the next to the last step towards the prize, was hoping that our parents would unwittingly give one of us the bag with the prized box (s). By now, our childish salivating was beginning to be too much to handle

– and true to childish form, it really became contentious competition between the two of us.

My goal was to never lose – and I wasn't about to start now. Being almost three years older, and a bit bigger (back then), I would muscle my way through the grocery bag and grab the Alphabet Cereal box. Now before you ask why would I be allowed to open a fresh box of cereal before its time? Let me explain – all I can tell you is that it was an art form, and I had mastered it, so much so, that I could get my little hand down in that box, grab the coveted prize, put the lid back together on the cereal and be gone in a hot flash. I shared that story with you hopefully to illustrate first, an understanding of human behavior as it pertains to knowing how good a reward can be and how much being rewarded means to us. Secondly, I wanted to draw your attention to the great lengths we commit when we are determined to be reward seekers. And finally, I wanted to offer a candid, but profound take on the necessity of doing what is required of us in order that we do in fact receive what is for us – that being a reward for our due diligence.

God, in all of His Omniscience, even today, desires that, we, His creations, develop that same, child-like passion and zeal to be rewarded by Him. I believe in the depths of my soul that God allows the things of this world to be paraded in front of us, partly to demonstrate that things and stuff, people, places and things, will all pass away – but only what we do for Christ will last. In other words, should you decide to follow Christ in your pursuits of success, there will be some challenges; there will be some disappointments; there will be some moments of doubt; there will be some unsettling circumstances that cause you to fear the unknown, the never before tried, the unthinkable, the un-imagined – but for your prevailing and persistent prayers and unyielding faith in our Father, God, still rewards you like non-other.

Devotional

I have often marveled at the various businesses that offer rewards cards. And even more intriguing, are the many different types of offerings that are presented to entice me to commit to saying, yes, I want to be a part of this club, or that program. The hotel chains have their approach, the airlines have theirs, the banks with their fancy credit card features, have theirs – and each can be extremely creative with the ability of dangling that proverbial carrot over one's head.

Each has a specific deadline with which to respond, along with a set of conditions to participating. My experience with all of the above for the past forty years, has been at best, hit and miss. Sometimes the timing just isn't right, or perhaps the conditions are a little too strict, making it more of an impossible challenge than a reward for coming on board. In essence, however, not any of them has the ability to reward us for our loyalty, in the same manner as, God. As a matter of fact, in their fine print, they remind us that they can rescind their offer without notification.

But here's what I love and respect about our God. Yes, God does make it clear that He's no respecter of person, and yes, He's very clear about the conditions by which we can receive our rewards for loyalty unto Him, such as repenting, trusting Him, and keeping the faith in times of trouble. However, God never changes – if He promised you something, you can rest assured that, what is for you, is for you. When God proclaims and decrees something, duly note that it shall come to pass. And, moreover, Whenever God postulates on any subject or discussion, He is incapable of lying. Unlike the companies that make these enticing offers, you have to be extremely careful to read the small print, because they have been known to lie; they have expiration dates that are often neatly tucked away in the fine print – but God plainly states that, "no man knows the day or the hour..." Matthew 24:36 (NLT). Simply put, while God is trying to bless you into success and reward you for your faithfulness and trustworthiness, He never runs out of gifts to reward you with, however, don't you wait too late to receive what is in store for you – get it while you can, because the best in Christ Jesus is yet to come!

Prayer

My hands, my heart, my head, and my soul are open to receive your rewards unto me, Oh, God. I thank you for thinking of me when you seek those to bless; I'm eternally grateful for your graciousness and your favor. And now, Father, please continue to use me for YOUR glory and my good, in the name of, Jesus, I pray, amen.

CHAPTER TWELVE

In The Meantime – S.O.A.R.

While preparing this final chapter, life was interrupted for me in a most astounding way. After I had labored over the necessary work to complete this book – for starters, I was given some very disturbing news about my health. It was around the third week of February when I began to feel some light discomfort in the center of my chest. It wasn't the obvious, often referred to pain as we've come to know as trouble symptoms with the heart. I just noticed that there was a little something off kilter in my chest – it was there as I attempted to lay down and sleep; it never left me as I would sit up to eat or watch television; it stayed with me as I attempted my daily walks – but it's presence never escalated into anything other than something that felt like it shouldn't be there – it just wasn't natural.

I'm one that is grateful to God for my body – I've always paid close attention to my body, therefore, I was accustomed to going to the doctor to get checked up and checked out. And after three days I determined that it was time to go and let the doctor have a look see to tell me what was going on. So, on Wednesday, February 25th, 2015, after undergoing several procedures (Echogram, EKG, Stress Test), it was determined that I was in desperate need of triple heart by-pass surgery. After being shuttled between three different hospitals for several days, on Wednesday, March 4th, the Chief Cardiologist came to my bedside and informed me that I didn't need a triple by-pass, but rather, because of the extensive blockage, I will be getting a quintuple by-pass – CABG 5, (Cardio Arterial By-pass Graft) pronounced, cabbage, just like the vegetable – and by the way, this procedure was not a common operation because apparently not many people have five major artery blockage as I had.

None the less, there I was, laid up in a hospital bed, life interrupted with no warning; stuck on chapter eleven of this book, with every intention of completing this writing assignment in no time at all, and my road to successfully completing a major chapter in my life thrust me into a quandary of "in the meantime." In other words, God deposited me in a place of complete silence from Him. The only thing that I remember about God while waiting to be operated on, was a powerful feeling of comfort and joy. I will never forget that feeling for as long as I shall live. Even though the doctors had told me that I was more than healthy enough to successfully endure the surgery, they also took great care to let me know that I could die on the operating table – but I didn't flinch; I just looked at the doctor and said, "let's get it done, I'm in God's hands and so are you!"

The nurses that took care of me as we all prepared for the big day were amazed at my faith, so much so that they began to talk to me about their personal walk with God, and how challenging it is at times, and they asked me to pray for them – imagine that, I'm lying in bed with needles and tubes coming out of me, praying for someone else. But, I had no fear, and I felt authorized and empowered by God Almighty to do His work, to be used by Him, even in the meantime – thank you nurse Campbell for letting me speak into your situation and for the praise party up on the tenth floor. And even though God was silent, I could feel His heavy presence, in particular whenever the team, and I do mean team of doctors would come around to pep me up and encourage me for the surgery, and they would always leave my bedside shaking their heads because God allowed me to take the lead and pep them up, as I reminded them to make sure that they followed God's lead in the operating room.

I soon found out that in the meantime, as we wait on God's will to be done, there is much for us to do, if only we be still and know that God is God all by Himself – God still sets the stage, assembles the participants, writes the script, directs the cast and produces the event, all with the right outcome, if we understand the blessing of, "in the meantime." I had some of the most compelling success as a minister, while being kept in the incubator of in the meantime – I never considered having a pity party, or waking in the wee hours of the night/morning, and crying out to God, asking, why me, God? None of that ever crossed my mind or entered my heart – I just felt the need for God to prove Himself, and was so honored that He chose me to do it for such a time as this.

It didn't take long for me to realize that I had begun to press towards making time to commune more with Christ – I put in a lot of time reflecting on the many Scriptures that talked about how He healed people, and inquired of their faith – yes, I soon realized that if I never passed the faith test before, I was well on my way of getting high marks on this un-expected exam. And it became apparent to me, more so now, than ever before, that when life gets interrupted by God, and we submit to His ways and His will, a higher level of consciousness for success kicks in – my soul began to rejoice in knowing that if I never accomplished another of my own goals in life, but as long as I stuck with God's flight plan, I would have experienced a kind of success unlike any other, and that was alright by me – because finally, I had begun to soar!

And by all intents and purpose, I realized that after all that I had been through, the failed attempts, the disappointments, and bouts of frustration and doubt, I had finally found my wings. Now, after everything that God had pre-destined for me, I had finally come to clearly, without doubt, hesitation, or reservation, gain clarity as to how and why, God was preparing me for success – I better understood that for everything and every time that I thought I was failing, God was preparing me for this moment in time, in spite of my fears and my human frailties – in my weakness, I became strong in His strength. And now, Isaiah's use of a metaphorical eagle, has helped me to prayerfully help you to glean the significance of the symbolic reference of such a bird and its characteristics, and its abilities.

Isaiah 40:31 – "But those who wait for the Lord [who expect, look for, and hope in Him] shall change and renew their strength and power; they shall lift their wings and mount up [close to God] as eagles [mount up to the sun]; they shall run and not be weary, they shall walk and not faint or become tired." Amplified Bible.

Jesus' declaration that his coming was not solely that we would merely have life, but have it in abundance, speaks succinctly to the wishes of God – God created each of us in His image – and He can do anything but fail! For the dreamers and doers – it's time to take flight and allow God's flight plan to lead and guide us to higher heights; taking us to people, places, and things, never imagined – now spread your wings and let's go soaring!

Therefore, in the meantime, as you hold your anxiety at bay, while patiently hoping and praying that God is working things out on your behalf – things that you have longed for ever since you can remember; the things that you went to college for with the aspirations of one day parlaying your equipping and preparation into a successful endeavor; the things that dreams are made of, yes, those things, are the things that are yet to come once you decide to spread your wings and take flight into your destiny – but first, you must enter into the process of dismissing your fear of flying, trusting and fully relying on God as you S.O.A.R. into your successful future.

S – Shake it off; O – Overcome all things; A – Accelerate your faith; R – Run hard until you take flight!

And that first step begins with you being willing to shake off whatever is binding you to your fear and preventing you from being free to fly. I remember growing up and overhearing the elders of the community, encouraging and admonishing each other to never let the devil win; you've got to shake him off like water running down a duck's back. Of, course it didn't make sense back then. But I can assure you that as I began to be introduced to the trials and pitfalls of what it meant to be grown and bear grown folk responsibilities while being flung head first into all of the problems that come with being grown – everything they said began to make sense with a great degree of clarity.

Realistically, what they were doing, was employing their survival techniques for such a time as they had to endure – dealing with the painful and brutal reality of Jim Crowism, segregation and racial hatred, were not casual occurrences, but instead, they were the norm, an understood way of life – and while in pursuit of the American dream of success to be had, it wasn't easy to come by. But what they had was something that the faithless would never come to understand – the elders, our fore parents possessed a hope that not even death could disappoint. They held fast to believing that their faith was overflowing with hope; they knew that sooner or later, their Concealed God would soon become their Revealed God – and His coming would honor every promise that was made on their behalf – success, in whatever context they prayed, would be theirs, for as long as they didn't cling to the need to carry the burden of trying to shoulder the doubters, hatemongers, blessing blockers – they knew how and why there was a need to just, shake it off – because when we shake it off, we're getting out of God's way and allowing Him to handle whatever trouble that betides us – Shake it Off!

Secondly, and equally important, is the need to overcome any and all things that hinder you from moving forward with the necessary conviction to succeed. Contrary to some beliefs, stuff is going to happen to you whether you want them to happen or not. I'm reminded of another old saying that rings loudly in my head – "life is 90% of what happens to you, and 10% of how you deal with it." Problematic for a lot of people, is that they go through life constantly focusing on and fussing about the 90%, rather than realizing that with God, that 10% reaction can be a major game changer for them, depending, however, in what manner it is utilized. The Bible clearly tells us that we have the ability to speak truth to power. In other words, we can confess and declare that failure is not an option! As believers and dreamers and doers, we can choose to speak with authority over our plans for a better life, or we can whisper words of defeat and doom into our own ears, while stifling and slowly killing any hope of succeeding at anything – God has given each of us a hope that transcends and overcomes all things, but to be successful, we must overcome every obstacle that rears its ugly head – and with Christ, we can, yes, we can do all things because in Christ, lies our strength.

Thirdly, Scripture tells us that, faith without works is dead. Basically, one way to embrace that text, is that as long as you're sitting around talking about what you are going to do, and yet, you've done nothing but talk about it, even as the years have crept by, then there's a great possibility that you will never do anything to advance your dreams into reality but talk about them – in essence, your talk has killed your dreams before God could ever breathe life into them. This is why it is tantamount that for every believer that harbors dreams of success, to understand the necessity of not becoming complacent with being a sedentary dreamer – one who sits around wishing and hoping, but never doing a single thing to accelerate the dream. I'm a witness to the truth about taking one step towards my heart's desires, and God moving on my behalf and taking two, three, four and sometimes even five steps on my behalf. If God has given you dreams of success, then accelerate your faith and not your fear; trust God to be constantly moving things around on your behalf – if He promised it, then He's already made provision for you –and you need only to trust Him and begin to accelerate your faith – trust me, He's waiting on you, and not the other way around.

In conclusion, once you are certain that you know, that you know, without a doubt that you understand what is required of you to succeed, and God has permitted you the privilege of being able to peek into the future and see what your success looks like – you should prepare yourself to run into your destiny with all of the energy, commitment, determination, and faith you can muster! Think on this – in spite of all that could abort your plans, God allows you to see each obstacle as Olympic hurdles assembled on the track field, and there you are in high stride, full throttle, running and leaping over each of them with other worldly bursts of energy and excitement; God has placed you in a position of promise that gives you the ability to see yourself hurdling down the track of life as you shake off the things that don't matter; He causes you to trust Him to help you to overcome all obstacles and constraints that affect your success; God is following behind you giving you the push that you need when you grow weary, as He becomes the wind beneath your wings, whereas allowing you to accelerate your faith and keep on going even when you don't feel like it; yes, my God, your God, is there as you run hard and forcefully into your destiny, – you push yourself to your limits, and He's there pulling you past all limitations – causing you to overcome the fear of flying, because success is now within your reach and all fear is gone.

Devotional

In the meantime is a place that occupies a certain hopeful space that causes us to sometimes wonder aloud if we are made of the stuff that gives us the necessary courage and tenacity to divorce ourselves from the temptation to take matters into our own hands. While I admit all of that is so very true, however, in the meantime is also a golden opportunity to see God in all of His providential splendor and glory. Beloved, there are countless lessons to be learned about the Omniscience of God, but here's one that is not difficult to obtain, and not terribly difficult to understand: God can do whatever God desires; He's had His eyes and heart on us from day one, with plans and opportunities abound, but because we can't handle the inside mysteries of His Divine workings, God will never expose His plan (s) to us before He's ready – God knows all about our proclivities to attempt to take matters into our own hands – therefore, God continues to display a "not now" attitude towards us, His creations, in order that He, while working in the meantime just for us, is certain that we are able to handle that which He has prepared with great detail and specificity just for us – developed, designed, and delivered, in the meantime, right on time.

Prayer

Dear God, today I simply ask that you continue to pour the gift of patience and trust into my spirit, that I may be totally and completely receptive to your Supreme Authority and Ability. Help me to become strong and bold in your foolproof word that your thoughts become my thoughts, and your desires for my life become my desires, that I may succeed according to your perfect will. I desire to detach myself from my own thinking, from my own plans and rest in the bosom of endless possibilities that exist in Your mysteries and hidden things, where you and you alone, can do the impossible, amen.

About the Author

Reverend Eddie L. Harris, Jr., is a teacher/preacher, author, motivational speaker, workshop facilitator/presenter, songwriter/producer, entrepreneur, visionary, scholar, and theologian. He was born in Sanford, Florida and reared in Montgomery, Alabama, Cleveland, Ohio, and Orlando, Florida, respectively. He is a retired Itinerant Elder of the African Methodist Episcopal Church. Pastor Harris is the Founder/Overseer of The Potter's Wheel Cathedral of Faith, a non-denominational faith center, located in Orlando, Florida. Pastor Harris also holds a Master of Divinity Degree from Turner Theological Seminary at the Interdenominational Theological Center, Atlanta, Georgia. He is also a proud member of Omega Psi Phi Fraternity, Inc., and he is available for motivational speaking, preaching engagements, readings, and interviews, and can be reached at:

eddieharris2212@gmail.com;

cell – 601-983-8439;

The Potter's Wheel Cathedral of Faith
– 6472 Long Breeze Road, Orlando, Florida 32810.